When Life Stinks, It's Time to Wash the Gym Clothes

Kelly Epperson

For my guys

Acknowledgments

My thanks to Mel, my first editor, for giving me a chance; and thanks to all the editors who run my column.

Thank you to anyone who has ever encouraged me in my writing - my parents, my family, my teachers, my friends, my divas, my chicks of the trade, Dave Barry, and Barry Manilow. Mostly, I thank you, the readers. Thanks for letting me be me.

Contents

[first published column]

Song Brings Back Memories

(May, 2001)

కావ్

It's spring! I'm driving with my windows down and the radio cranked. I feel young and carefree. For a while I forget that I'm a thirty-something mother of two. That is until the boy at the fast food drive-up window hands me my food and calls me "ma'am."

Exactly when did I become a "ma'am?" Perhaps the fact that I was driving a minivan tipped him off. Oh well, I enjoyed my fries, and turned up the radio a little louder.

A song by .38 Special came on. Instant time warp to 1981. Holy crooked river, can it possibly be twenty years? I was a junior in high school and my boyfriend was a senior. Curt was a good guy, funny and smart.

We met while working at Arby's. We rarely had customers. Everyone hung out at the McDonald's across the street. Young romance blossomed while slicing roast beef and making jamocha shakes. Anyone who found me attractive in that ugly brown polyester uniform will always hold a soft spot in my heart.

Our high school campus had over 1,000 kids walking the halls, and that was only juniors and seniors. I didn't know Curt before we started working together. The first time I saw him at school, he was wearing ripped jeans and a black concert t-shirt. *Oh my gosh, Curt's a hood!* (What word do they use now?)

He actually was a great guy, so hearing this song made me think that it would be nice to call him up. "Hey, I heard a song today that made me think of you. How the heck are you? Married? Kids? How is your life going?" But of course, I can't do that.

First of all, I don't know where he is. He may still be in the area, but our paths have not crossed. We didn't have mutual friends so I'm not in touch with anyone who would know his story. But the real reason that I don't pick up the phone is that it is not the socially correct thing to do in our society.

If I were thinking about an old female friend, I would be a real pal to get in touch to reminisce. It would probably make both our days to reconnect and relive some fun times. It just isn't the same when dealing with the opposite sex.

My husband may not have a jealous bone in his body, but I sure do. If some old girlfriend of his rang him up after twenty years "just to say hi," I would be convinced that she had ulterior motives. Such things have been known to happen, y'know.

So I kept my innocent curiosity to myself. I don't really know what I would say anyway. I was just having an 80's flashback. It was nice while it lasted. But I know who I can call. The guys at the classic rock radio station playing my tunes. Thanks for the memories.

The Music In Me

(June, 2001)

Buried somewhere amid suitcases and sentimental treasures in our basement is an old crate of record albums. I've made The Man of the Place drag it along with us through every housing move.

We don't have a turntable to play vinyl records, but I won't part with them. My sons know the albums are ancient artifacts from Mama's youth, back in the days of no VCRs and when a person had to get up off the couch to change the TV channel. I grew up without a computer or Nintendo, but somehow I survived.

In our modern-day world, some tech-genius had the brilliant (that is, money-making) idea to put LPs onto CDs.

"Mom, what does LP mean?"

"I think it stands for Long Playing."

"What about CD?"

"Compact disk."

"Why does it say CD at the bank? They sell music?"

"No, honey, that's a different kind of CD."

The Man of the Place appreciates the tech-genius when he's jamming to his Triumph Classics. However, he feels differently when it comes to my musical smorgasbord. Van Halen and Prince. Pat Benatar and Queen. Blondie and Styx. All peas in a pod, right? Actually, my hubby doesn't mind most of my selections. He only cringes when I get out Barry Manilow or the Carpenters. Just another cruel and unusual punishment of being married to me.

Our old faves have some similarities. Listen to the lyrics. Triumph sings: She's lying on her bed, pulls the covers overhead, and turns her little radio on. She's had a rotten day so she hopes the deejay is gonna play her favorite song. From the Carpenters: When I was young, I'd listen to the radio, waiting for my favorite songs. When they played, I'd sing along. It made me smile.

Same sentiment; different presentation.

I must admit that buying the Carpenters' CD made me smile. I was banished to the bedroom to enjoy my new purchase. I cranked my boom box (okay, I guess one does not really "crank" the Carpenters), and surprisingly I remembered every word to songs I had long forgotten. I grabbed my hairbrush microphone to lip sync for my boys. They went scurrying for Daddy.

"Help! Mom is acting really weird!"

My guys were surprised to hear Karen and Richard's version of "Sing." They had thought I made up the song. Whenever my younger son tells me that I can't sing (daily), I answer back in song: Sing! Sing a song. Sing out loud. Sing out strong. Make it simple to last your whole life long. Don't worry that it's not good enough for anyone else to hear, just sing, sing a song."

That's my motto because I know where my talent does not lie. I sing out loud and strong in the privacy of my own home, but my boy is right. I can't sing and I accept that fact of life. Maybe that is why I enjoy music so much. Those who can't sing appreciate those who can.

Maybe someday, I will get the chance to teach a music appreciation class. (Look out, the samples will be eclectic). For now, I'll share my varied tastes with my children. My parents' 1950's music was part of my childhood. My boys in turn will share their musical heritage with their kids. It's hard to imagine, but someday their children will be subjected to "Who Let The Dogs Out." Some traditions must go on.

The Realities Of Child Rearing

(June, 2001)

જેન્જી

I've learned one truth in my life so far: My kids will make a liar out of me every time.

Before we had children, I was an expert on child rearing. No kid of mine would talk back to me like that. No kid of mine would hit. My children wouldn't have identical toys – what's up with that?

During my first pregnancy, I believed I would only breast feed and use cloth diapers. I would limit my toddlers' television to 30 minutes a day. I would make a healthy breakfast every morning.

Then my children were born. Two in a row. I tried disposable diapers and bottle liners. Hallelujah. The clouds parted and angels sang. Or maybe it was me. Convenience was the key to my new life as a mom.

With a toddler and a baby, I discovered the TV/VCR was an essential piece of equipment, equal to the crib or high chair. Ask any mom of young ones, which would she rather part with: all her kitchen appliances or the video player? No bookie in Vegas would take that bet.

15

"You want another video, honey? Sure, pop it in." We didn't OD on *Barney* like many a neighborhood tot. We kept a varied and well-stocked video cabinet. 30 minute limit? Yeah, each hour.

I did make sure my children always got a healthy breakfast before we left the house. Well, breakfast anyway. And not exactly before we left the house.

"We don't have time for waffles this morning. That's why God invented Pop Tarts; they're easy to eat in the van. Now where are your shoes?"

Oh, and that identical toy issue; my boys do know how to share, but in the interest of peace (of those poor souls around us), I have been known to trade in a Happy Meal toy or two. Yes, for the black car with the purple streak, the one just like brother's. Hmm....

My children have talked back in disrespect and yes, even rolled their eyes at me. I don't tolerate it, but it's happened. My boys have hit each other. I don't tolerate it, but it's happened.

You'd think I would have learned. When my boys were small, I watched parents with older kids running every night to sports, dance class, Scouts, music lessons, etc. I vowed I wouldn't be one of "those parents."

Duh, silly me. Liar, liar, pants on fire. My boys are school age now and we are a family on the go. The boys will do anything and everything that mom and dad cough up the bucks for and drive them to.

We parents eventually force them to choose between activities so we can have a night off to stay home and prepare a healthy supper. Waffles, perhaps.

This parenting gig is definitely learned as I go along. It was easy to be smug when I was in the BC (Before Children) years, but now that I am in the trenches of raising kids, it's a whole new story. And I'm still learning. The real truth in parenting is to never say never. The teenage years lurk ahead. Need I say more?

Looking For A Lost Love

(July, 2001)

&*&

I'm searching for a treasure from my past and I can't find it. It must have gotten tossed in the Goodwill box during our last move. I try to live with no regrets, but if I've discarded my necklace, I regret it.

It was one of a kind: a sparkling rhinestone beauty spelling ANDY GIBB.

Andy was my first true love. Oh sure, there had been others before him. David Cassidy for a week. Donny Osmond for much longer. But, as Donny sang, it was only "puppy love." With Andy, it was the real deal. I wasn't a little girl anymore. I was mature now. I was in junior high.

The hot pink walls of my bedroom were covered with Andy Gibb posters. I had his album (or did he have two?) and I thought he was gorgeous. My friend Jeannie was a fellow Andy fan. Her parents took us to the Wisconsin State Fair to see Andy Gibb IN CONCERT.

Pre-teen girls were screaming and crying. It was as exciting as a Beatles or Elvis performance. We befriended other hysterical girls there. Two fans that lived near the fairgrounds had taken pictures of Andy riding a horse before the concert. We became pen pals for a month and they sent me a copy of the Andy on horseback photo. It's in my official Andy Gibb scrapbook.

Our seats for the concert were in the back of the grandstand. Jeannie's dad and his camera ventured to the front row for some amazing up-close shots. If I could find the photos, you'd be impressed. Andy sweating. Andy with his shirt unbuttoned. Andy with his shirt off.

Now that the youngest of the Brothers Gibb is no longer with us on this earth, those pictures could probably fetch some dollars on eBay, but I won't sell them. That is if I could locate them. Did my Andy pictures get put in the Goodwill bag too?

I don't remember exactly when my passion for Andy faded. I guess I moved on to real boys who could kiss me back. I do recall that I was truly saddened by his untimely death. I mourned him with the gals from work. They didn't share my girlhood intensity for the man, but got a kick out of my pictures, scrapbook, and necklace.

A recent Bee Gees television special got me thinking about my lost love Andy. Although the Man of the Place would disown me, I thought it would be a fun conversation starter to wear my necklace again. If it would still fit around my neck, I don't know. It may have to work as an ankle bracelet.

But I guess we'll never know. Some bargain hunter at the Goodwill store may have snatched up my trinket. Or worse, it could be in the garbage dump. I can't think that thought. I'll keep looking. It just may turn up.

In the meantime, I can revisit my other school girl crush. Donny Osmond is looking fine in his loincloth in the lead role in *Joseph and the Amazing Technicolor Dreamcoat*. I have the musical on video. Come on over and join me, girls. Don't forget your scrapbooks.

The One About TV Guide

(July, 2001)

൧൦൬

Good writers should be well read. That's why I subscribe to *TV Guide*. It's my weekly source of the latest in pop culture. It's also a handy purse-size publication that I can take along for those long waits at the orthodontist's office.

Actually, on our last visit to the brace place, three of us waiting mothers were toting the most recent *Reader's Digest*. It too is portable, but is a little more "respectable" reading. I doubt my English professors would want to be seen in public doing the *TV Guide* crosswords puzzle. Three letters: ___ in the Family. Five letters: As the _____ Turns. *TV Guide* has a hotline to call just in case you get stumped.

My *TV Guide* may never leave the house (it fits so nicely on the toilet tank), but it is a happy mail day when it arrives. Magazines beat bills any day, and I do like to time myself to see how fast I can finish the crossword. My *TV Guide* gives me fun morsels of useless trivia and the scoop of what is happening in TV Land. Hey wait, isn't that a channel now?

When I was young, we had a (gasp!) black and white set with no cable. We had only one TV and had to watch what my dad liked. We suffered through *Hee-Haw* every Saturday night. ("Gloom, despair, and agony on me. Deep dark depression, excessive misery. If it weren't for bad luck, I'd have no luck at all...") Why do such things remain lodged in my brain? I still can't drive through a tiny town without exclaiming the population and "Sal-loot!"

When my dad was at work, we got our share of *Gilligan's Island* (another song permanently in my DNA) and other junk TV. Anyone in my age demographic can view the first ten seconds of a *Brady Bunch* episode and identify it: the one where Marcia's nose gets hit with the football ("Oh my nose!"); the one where Marcia has a crush on Davey Jones; the one where Jan is fed up playing second fiddle to Marcia (in unison now: "It's always Marcia, Marcia, Marcia!").

I spend more time now reading about TV than watching it. We don't have HBO, but I know all about the Sopranos. I don't watch daytime TV, but I can tell you everything about *Passions*. My *TV Guide* informed that the NBC peacock was going to be a butterfly until the artist changed his mind. That little gem could pay off someday when I'm in the hot seat facing Regis.

Don't get me wrong. Our TV is on all the time here. Sports. Bond Week. Movies for Guys Who Like Movies. It's a no-brainer that I'm not the one in control of the control. It's a genetic condition. Males of the human species are born with a thumb poised for clicking. The dexterity develops as they get older.

Eventually they reach the age where they fall asleep with the remote in their hand. They only awaken when it is gently slipped from their fingers. It's part of the evolution theory. The caveman was always clutching a club. Modern man, a remote control.

Modern woman relies on her *TV Guide*. Since I'm not the one flipping through the channels, how else would I know that Nick at Nite is doing Pop-Up Brady? Favorite episodes of the *Brady Bunch* with trivia in bubbles popping up over the heads of Peter, Alice and Bobby. I bet Tiger will be included too.

Now that certainly is must-see TV. I just might tune in. If I can get control of the remote.

Job Hazards Of Parenting

(August, 2001)

❧❧

I should be germ-free by the time this goes to print, but it might not be a bad idea for you to go wash your hands. With soap. (Sorry, it's a habit. Am I the only parent that has to explain what "wash hands" means?)

My little darlings share everything, including the stomach flu. They recently kept me up all night with dueling puke buckets. It suddenly became clear why we decided two kids were enough. I don't know how I could comfort three sick kids. And I need my sleep.

Within a couple days, they bounced back, as kids do. Then I started to feel queasy. "If I get sick, you're in big trouble," I warned, but it didn't work. Come nightfall, it was my turn. For the first time since we moved to this old house, I was wishing for a bathroom right next to my bedroom.

As I lay on the bathroom floor, trying to sleep in between the waves of vicious flu bugs squeezing my intestines through their vise grips, my mind wandered back to when my boys were babies. The early days of my mommy experience revolved around the miracles of a baby:

how much laundry a tiny person can create and how much formula can be spit across the family room.

Do you remember the moment when you felt that you had earned your wings as a parent? For some fathers, maybe it was changing a poopy diaper. For me, it was getting puked on.

I'm not referring to infant spit up. I knew that went with the territory. My scent for two years was Essence of Similac. My babies urped up more than they ate, but still gained weight; a medical mystery.

My defining moment, the badge of motherhood, was my older son's first official regurgitation. He hurled all over me; and I didn't care. That's when I knew that I was a bona fide parent.

He was a toddler and eating real food. The first upchuck of solids is a scary ordeal. I needed to comfort him. That meant him being in my arms and my shirt being the vomit vat.

"It's okay, honey, you'll be all right." It would not have mattered to me if I was wearing a mink coat. My sole concern was my little boy.

If being in love means never having to say you're sorry, being a mom means taking a barf bath and saying,

"I'm sorry. I'm so sorry you are sick." We moms constantly apologize for things we have no control over.

Fast forward to our present day home. Instead of calm, reassuring words, I now scream, "Run! Get to the bathroom! The toilet! The toilet!"

Once the sickie is safely to the flusher, I'll rub a back and offer soothing words. I haven't lost all compassion. They're big boys now and know what to do when the tummy bug strikes. And now they know how to comfort Mama too.

I've moved from the bathroom floor to my bed. My sweeties bring me a stuffed animal and ask if I want a puke bucket. They pat my hand and say, "I'm sorry. I'm sorry you're sick, Mommy."

Fashion Statements/Fashion Questions

(September, 2001)

৵৽৻

It's time to skim the back-to-school ads and check out the latest fashion. Look at that poor model. Her sweater is two sizes too small. It must have shrunk in the dryer. Her belly button's hanging out. Poor thing, she's wearing hand-me-downs that don't fit.

When I was young, if my mom would have bought me a sweater that revealed my navel, I would have shipped her off to the loony bin. I didn't expose my belly button then and I don't think the world wants to see my two-babies-in-two-years belly now. But those ads aren't targeted at me. Hair color, age-defying make up, and control top pantyhose are aimed at my demographic.

Without daughters in my household, I don't keep up with the latest trends. Some looks from my teenage years are still ingrained though. I refuse to wear socks with sandals. That combination looks fine on my children, but I just can't do it. When I grew up, only dorks wore socks with sandals. Today there is obviously a different standard for dorkiness.

I just may be a contender. I'm no slob in my old age, but these days I choose comfort over cute. I'd prefer to wear jammies and slippers everywhere, but then my boys would be shipping me off to the loony bin.

I've never been a slave to fashion. I considered myself its master, creating my own sense of style. Sure, I followed some fads. I wore plaid super-wide bell-bottoms in 4th grade and tripped over my own bell-bottom, breaking my arm. It was a high price to pay for fashion.

When I was in high school, I would not be caught dead wearing a hat or my hood, no matter how low the mercury dipped. My mother predicted that I would in fact be caught dead, frozen to death, but my hair not getting mussed was my priority. I still don't wear hats.

In college, I had a penchant for wearing wild earrings. My hair had the 80's punk strip and a tail. My roomie and I would paint our fingernails every night to complement our outfits for the next day. White with red stripes. Polka dots. A different color for each nail. We weren't concerned about being in vogue. It was funky and we had fun.

After graduation, I worked in the conservative accounting world. Business suits, little pearl earrings, one color nails. Bor-ing. Then came the mommy years. For some working mothers, a soft scarf around the neck or a lovely brooch on the lapel completed the outfit. My wardrobe staple was the burp cloth dramatically draped over the shoulder. It came in one go-with-anything color: stained.

For better or worse, fashion is cyclical. I see young gals today in flare leg jeans. I hope they don't trip. Maybe in twenty years I'll be donning a burp rag again. I won't be buying a belly sweater any time soon, but maybe I could go do some sit-ups. On second thought, I think I'll just paint my nails.

Diary of September 11

(September, 2001)

හ⊰

Tuesday, September 11: Oh my God. Oh my God. Words of shock, horror, disbelief. Words of prayer and supplication. The sight was unbelievable. The reporters' comments seemed trite. We overuse our adjectives so much that when an event is truly shocking, words can't fully express the emotion. In reality, no words could describe a tragedy that the mind cannot fully comprehend.

My immediate reaction was to pray selfish prayers. Thank you that my family is safe. Thank you that we live in the Midwest far removed from possible targets. Thank you that my husband is home from his trip and not stranded across the country.

I prayed for the victims in New York and the Pentagon. I prayed for all the people on the hijacked planes. I prayed for the families that lost a loved one. I prayed for President Bush and all the military advisors. I prayed for the right words to tell my children that America had been attacked. How could I explain such evil exists in the world and still reassure them that they were safe?

It never occurred to me to pray for the attackers.

I knew the raw emotion I was feeling would fade in the days to come. I prayed that I would evaluate my priorities daily and live my life focusing on what really matters.

Wednesday, September 12: I awoke from a deep sleep and momentarily forgot that our world had been turned upside-down. Made breakfast, packed lunches. The tooth fairy had come in the night even though all flights had been grounded. Our outward life seemed unchanged.

I walked my boys to school and had to fight the urge to hug every kid in line. We are indeed blessed. The blue skies and beautiful fall day belied the tragedy of New York and Washington. Again I spent the day glued to the TV. I couldn't focus on work. I allowed myself to weep.

Thursday, September 13: I thought I'd try denial. I didn't turn on the TV. I took what little work I'd accomplished to the office. Everyone was busy as usual. It was comforting and yet, disconcerting.

Yes, life goes on. But life is different now. I work for The Literacy Council. Our mission is to help people learn to

read. I still believe that is worthwhile work. If not, I think I
would have quit on the spot.

Friday, September 14: I watched the National Prayer
Service and tried to write. I wore red, white and blue. My flag
waved in the breeze. I dug out candles to light.

Still struggling with my emotions and my words, I
send this off to print. We have been reminded in a dreadfully
dramatic way of the brevity and uncertainty of life. I have lost
my innocence. It saddens me that our children, so young,
have lost theirs.

I am dazed and confused, but still holding fast to my
ideals. I know in the very core of my being that goodness
and evil are not equal. Light repels the dark. Love is stronger
than hate.

In all corners of the earth, love is stronger than hate.

We Make 'Em And Break 'Em

(December, 2001)

৯৽৵

It's that time of year again. Big or small, we make them and we break them. New Year's resolutions are not my thing. This year, I'll cut right to the chase and make resolutions I know I'll break.

I resolve to make my bed every day. I will dust and vacuum with a smile. I will clean the bathroom without telling my family to please ask if they can go next door. I will not yell, "I just cleaned and I want it to stay that way!"

I resolve to exercise four times a week. I will share the DoubleStuff Oreos and not hide a package in the cupboard just for me. I resolve to make a hot breakfast for my family every morning. I will throw out the phone number to the pizza place. I will cook supper every night and top it off with a home-baked dessert.

I resolve to never utter a swear word ever again. I will not call my children little dorks. I will not tell the dog to shut up. I resolve to get my film developed as soon as I take it out of the camera. I will put those photos immediately into albums or scrapbooks. I will organize and file the last three years worth of photographs. I will learn how to use the new digital camera and timely email pictures to people as promised.

I resolve to sew loose buttons and ripped pajama pants right away. I will not let the laundry sit in the dryer for three days. I resolve to sort through the clutter on the kitchen counter instead of moving the piles from kitchen to dining room and back again.

I resolve to send birthday cards on time. I will not buy a belated birthday greeting no matter how funny I think it is. I resolve to learn to play the piano. I will learn a second language. Pig Latin counts. Ig-pay atin-lay ounts-cay.

I resolve to never buy anything for myself when I'm on a shopping errand. I will resist temptation. I will resist temptation. I will resist temptation. I resolve to never repeat things three times.

I resolve to think big. I will climb a mountain, ski a mountain, paint a mountain. I will paint holding the brush between my teeth. I resolve to learn how to play Nintendo with my boys. I will watch football with my husband and yell at the TV.

I resolve to clip coupons and actually use them. I will clean out my purse every night. I will save for a rainy day. I resolve to get manicures, take bubble baths, and never again will I cut my own hair. I will shave my legs in the dead of winter.

I resolve to make resolutions next year that I can keep.

Mysteries of IQ Testing Revealed

(January, 2002)

Ⅎℕ

I've always wondered about the IQ test. Where do you go to take it? Who made up the test? Is it graded on a curve?

I decided to go online to seek the answers to these questions. I got sidetracked though; AOL was offering a free IQ test. I was beckoned with "Madonna scored a 140, Bill Gates a 160...How Smart Are You?" In the name of research, I had to give it a try. Okey dokey, here goes nothing.

"The test will synthesize your IQ by evaluating 12 types of intelligences (I didn't know intelligence could be made plural; in fact, my spellchecker is turning red and "intelligences" is not in my dictionary. But I digress, back to the test), such as pattern recognition, arithmetic, logic, spatial skills and processing speed." They said 12 types. What are the other seven? My inquiring mind wants to know.

The test consists of 32 true or false questions, and takes an average of 12 minutes to complete. I entered my age and clicked to begin. I didn't time myself, but I finished well under 12 minutes. Eureka! I have "above average intelligence"! I knew it!

Wait a minute. Madonna and Bill Gates scored better than I did. I took the test again. This time I clicked as quickly as possible (how quickly you can click is directly related to your IQ; who knew?). I answered "true" to all 32 questions. My score was 116. I still have above average intelligence! I knew it!

In order to support my theory, which is…oh, yeah, that I'm no dummy, I tested again. Clicking quickly, I answered all questions as "false." The score, 99, is "average intelligence." My intelligence is fading fast. Or maybe it's my clicking ability.

Perhaps age is a factor in scoring. I entered age 17 and tested again. Answering all true, I scored 118. Two points higher. Maybe because I'm younger or maybe I was quicker with the clicker. Another go-round, age 17, answering all false. I scored 97; two points lower than the previous all false score. Hmm, these results are confusing my hypothetical hypothesis.

Maybe aging would help. I entered age 87 and ran through it again. Entering all true, I was back to the same score of 116. Entering all false, again a score of 99. Is this the same IQ test Einstein took? How fast was he able to click?

As final evidence to support my conclusion, which is still inconclusive, I took the test one more time. I entered my true age and clicking quickly, I tried to remember the answers from the first time when I actually read the questions. I scored 159! I'm "gifted!" I knew it!

The range for "above average intelligence" is 111-128 and "gifted" is 144-160. What about scores 129-143? Are those folks categorized as "slightly above above-average?" "Not quite gifted, but pretty darn close?" "Too smart for their own good?"

I didn't order the full analysis of my score for the low, low price of only $9.95. Maybe it would explain the 12 types of intelligences and the score ranges. Maybe it would answer all my questions about the Intelligence Quotient. Or maybe it simply says, "You just wasted $9.95. It doesn't take a genius to see that."

Time Flies, No Matter What

(May, 2002)

୬ଡ଼ଔ

"Like sands through the hourglass, so are the days of our lives." The hole in the middle of my hourglass must have widened because the sand is falling through at record pace.

Here we are, mid-May of 2002. Wasn't it just last week we were celebrating the new millennium? Heck, I still remember the bicentennial. But sand by sand, time keeps passing. My babies are big boys and my first nephew is graduating high school this weekend.

Blake was in diapers when we first met and Saturday he'll be in cap and gown. He's always been a good boy, but now I'll have to refer to him as a fine young man. I still picture the adorable tike who was the ring bearer (the ringmaster, as he put it) at our wedding. My husband is cute, but he was no match for a dimpled four-year-old in a tux. I married the Man of the Place so I could become "Aunt Kelly."

Now Blake is heading to college. In a few short years, his brother Riley will graduate also. Then the rest of the cousin gang will follow. Gulp. If my nieces and nephews are growing up, what does that mean for my boys?

It means that they too are growing up. And I am growing older. The older I get, the more I think time flies whether I am having fun or not. It's a sure sign of aging just to say the phrase "time flies."

With modern technology and all the gizmos in the movies, there should be a way to prolong the fun. There should be a button I can push to lengthen the good days and fast forward through the crabby days when my boys bicker and declare, "I don't like my brother and never want to play with him ever again."

But the sands keep slipping by. Last year I freaked when I realized my first born son would graduate in ten years. This year I am facing the fact that in ten years, my baby will graduate too.

Ten years; one short decade. There are days when that feels like an eternity, but when I look back on how quickly the last ten years went, I have a hunch the next ten will zip along just as fast.

When I am frustrated with endless laundry and a constant mess in the kitchen, I remind myself that I am halfway through my child rearing years. When the Man of the Place complains about Lego's and baseball cards strewn all over the floor, I remind him that we only have ten years left with kids in the house.

His reply: "If they live that long." God willing, they will. They're good boys who will grow into fine young men, just like their cousins. Sure, I have moments when I'd like to flip my hourglass over or at least knock it on its side to slow it down, but that's not how life works. So I envision each grain of sand passing through the middle of the hourglass crystallizing into a beautiful memory.

When my allotted sands have all passed to the bottom, my hourglass will be full of sparkling diamonds of time well spent.

I Never Can Say Goodbye

(June, 2002)

I'm singing again. This time I'm Michael Jackson; the original version that we all knew and loved: big fro, wide nose, brown skin. He was the dancing machine with the high voice. I always feel the need to spin when singing like Michael. I'm still working on the moonwalk.

"I never can say goodbye. No no, no no no. I never can say goodbye." That's all of his song that I need right now. I use snippets of lyrics to suit my mood. I take bits and pieces and add my own words. My children never know if a song is real or "mommified."

The truth is I never can say goodbye. Like all good Americans, when something is difficult for me, I avoid it. Goodbyes fit into that category.

I have read that children make friends in three minutes, but adults take three years. At this stage in my life, I don't want to wait that long. I have a co-worker, Minta, who I immediately clicked with. She has a daughter named Kelly so I figured she must be all right.

We haven't been friends long. She moved here less than a year ago. I think we crossed the bridge from "friendly" to "friend" when I invited her family to join us for Thanksgiving dinner. I was having a house full of people and three more wouldn't make a difference.

Minta informed me that her traveling-salesman husband is actually a chef by trade, and he was whipping up a gourmet feast for the three of them. My menu of Stovetop stuffing and a Butterball in a bag surely would have knocked their socks off.

Even though Minta had never read Laura Ingalls Wilder books or Nancy Drew mysteries, I decided that she still had the makings of a life-long friend. However, her galloping gourmet hubby took a job in Miami and now I am faced with having to say goodbye.

I try to be a positive person, but Minta doesn't have to try. It's just her nature. I'll miss her sunny side up attitude and how she would show up at my office with Cokes and a smile, just like a commercial.

Minta left me her tea plant that the movers wouldn't take. She's had that thing for 22 years. If it lasts 22 days in my care, it will be a miracle. I think I will name it Mint-tea. I might even read Little House stories to it.

I'm not a child anymore so if I feel comfortable with someone in three minutes, I want to keep that friend. I don't want to say goodbye, so I don't. I say we'll keep in touch. We have telephone, email, and good old-fashioned letter writing (yes, some of us still use that antiquated form of communication).

I say farewell; that's a lovely word, sincere and to the point. I imitate Arnold Schwarzenegger: Hasta la vista, baby. I sing from the *Sound of Music*, hand movements included: So long, farewell, auf Wiedersehen, good night. I quote Tigger: TTFN, ta-ta for now.

I say many things, but I never can say goodbye.

Are You Wearing The Wrong Size?

(August, 2002)

ক্ষ

News flash: According to JCPenney, 8 out of 10 women are wearing the wrong bra size. Who knew? And how does JCPenney know? Are their surveillance cameras equipped with x-ray vision? Do trained security guards stop customers at the exit? "Excuse me, miss, you weren't shoplifting, but you are wearing the wrong bra size."

The JCPenney National Bra Fit Event was held in June. How did this event fall under the radar of our local news crews? If it's a national event, shouldn't CNN reporters be on the scene with a tape measure? "Sorry, ma'am, you really should be wearing a 36C." I hate to think I'm wearing cup size Nearly Needing a Bra when my true size is Not Even Close.

If 8 out of 10 women are wearing the wrong size, odds are I'm in that statistic. Who are the two women wearing the correct size? Do they know it or is it just a fluke? Maybe they were alerted and attended the National Bra Fit Event.

The rest of us gals will have to wait until next year, stuck wearing our ill-fitting bras. Or we could shop the JCPenney catalog. The current book devotes 36 pages to bras, but nowhere do I find instructions to get the right fit. The bra makers want us to buy the wrong size. They figure we'll just keep buying bras.

So many choices are available. We have the Amazing Bra, the Wonder Bra, and the Miracle Bra. My sister-in-law bought a water-filled bra she claims could create cleavage for even me. (The Cleavage for Even Me Bra?) I never bothered to try it. I was afraid I'd hug someone and spring a leak.

There's lingo to learn in the bra industry: Underwire, seamless, plunge, demi, padded, molded, soft cups, strapless, racer back, convertible, full figure support, minimizers, and push-ups. For me, a push-up is orange sherbet in a paper tube with a stick. Underwire? Something to do with my son's braces. Demi? She's a celebrity who used to be married to Bruce Willis.

Too much on the market causes confusion. We need to return to a simpler time. I could market a new line of retro bras: Get back your girlish figure. One size fits all. Buy any cup size and receive a free box of tissues. Kleenex™ – safer than surgery.

The "Stuff-It Bra" may not succeed in all the current competition. The name isn't as pretty as the Magic Lift Bra. Some practical bras have survived. The Eighteen-Hour Bra has been around forever. It's about due for a modern name change, maybe the 24/7 Bra.

Now that I'm aware of it, I won't let the National Bra Event slip by me next year. A national event warrants a new outfit and in this case, a new bra. Just My Size. JCPenney will then have to change their stats to say 7 out of 10 are wearing the wrong bra size. I'll be there. Cross My Heart.

Diana, England's Rose

(August, 2002)

∂∾∾

Five years ago August 31, the world was united in shock and grief. Diana, Princess of Wales, was dead. I vividly remember my learning of her death. The headline of the Sunday morning paper stunned me with the news. "It can't be. I can't believe it," I repeated over and over. My older son asked me what was wrong. I told him that a lady died.

"Do we know her?"

"Not really."

"Then why are you so upset?"

Good question. I didn't know. My grief surprised me. Taking the newspaper into the bathroom, I locked the door and read in privacy. I cried. I felt odd that I was so shaken. Then I turned on the TV. I was not alone in my grief. The entire world was shaken.

The only story on all the channels was the death of Diana. The paparazzi chase and car crash had been reported Saturday night, but I had not known. If I had, I may have maintained an all-night vigil awaiting news of her survival.

But she did not survive. Every woman I know, of every age and background, mourned her. Diana was young, beautiful, and world famous, someone seemingly able to defy death. No one could have predicted that the world's unceasing fascination with her would factor into her death.

I turned off the television. All Diana had wanted was to enjoy some moments of a private life. In her death, I thought it best to leave her alone. A week later, I did get up early to watch the televised funeral. As soon as it was over and Peter Jennings began reiterating the high points of the eulogy, I turned the TV off. She's gone; let her rest in peace.

My memory of the Princess includes an actual Royal Sighting. It sounds very impressive to say she and I attended the same concert. We were in the same place at the same time. The summer of 1985, I went to the Live Aid concert at London's Wembley Stadium. Diana was with Charles in a box seat. I was in the crowd of 70,000 with a scalped ticket and no seat. The Royal Couple was announced and they waved. I returned to college telling everyone I partied with Chuck and Di.

We were all on a first name basis with Diana. We knew of her unhappy marriage, her fabulous gowns, and her role as England's goodwill ambassador. She lent her celebrity to many charitable causes and connected with people of all races, gender, and status. Princess Di was dubbed the People's Princess and the worldwide outpouring of grief was unprecedented. The sad fact is that Diana didn't know how much she was loved.

By all accounts, the title she cherished above all others was that of mum to her boys. The images of her beloved sons walking behind the funeral procession were the most heartbreaking. Diana would not see her sons grow up.

Diana was dead at 36 years old. We paid attention to where she went, who she was with, and what she wore. We should've paid more attention to her actions. Diana helped raise funds for more than 100 charities. She once said, "The biggest disease this world suffers from…is people feeling unloved. I can give love." That she did.

An enduring legacy, and in that respect, we can all strive to live like a princess.

Reality TV? Not For Me

(November, 2002)

৵৽৻

I don't watch reality TV therefore I must be out of touch with the real world. I'm not talking about *The Real World* which airs on MTV. I've never seen it, but I do know that it was the first of the "reality" shows. The MTV producers took a bunch of young people, strangers, and had them shack up together, with cameras on them all the time. It was a radical idea at the time.

I certainly wouldn't welcome television cameras into my house and I already know the people who live with me. We're the average American family, burping and farting around the dinner table. At least the censorship committee wouldn't have to bleep out every other word like on *The Osbournes.* I've never seen that show either. Maybe it's entertaining and heartwarming. Maybe it's profanity-laced bulls*%#. It's a ratings winner and that's all the powers-that-be care about.

I don't have anything against the *Survivor* series; I've just never watched it. Ever. At this point, I want to be the only person on the planet who has never seen an episode.

Maybe if they do a segment called *Survivor: Pecatonica, IL,* I'll break my streak and tune in.

The show that rankled me was *Temptation Island.* The people who go on these shows care about an ounce of fame more than anything else. "Hey honey, let's go away and be surrounded by people who want to break us up. We'll get to watch each other be tempted. And so will all of America." That is the only part that registers with them: All of America will be watching. Except me.

I just shake my head, but the shows keep coming. We're on round two of *The Bachelor,* with the third season already in production. The first dream guy turned out to be a wannabe actor and a jerk, but he got press and so did the show. The new bachelor is supposed to be a nice, genuine guy. And twenty-five beauties lined up to willingly face public humiliation. I just don't get it.

America Online lets you vote on who the bachelor should pick as his bride. "Aaron is narrowing down the field of bachelorettes competing to be his bride." Competing to be the bride. How romantic. What stories will the bachelor and his bride tell their children?

"Mommy, how did you meet Daddy?"

"Well, sweetie, I had to audition. I made the first round of cuts and I had to wear a swimsuit and get my teeth whitened for the camera. Then Daddy and I had deep, meaningful discussions on primetime television and he picked me."

"So you won Daddy at a beauty pageant?"

"Yes, that's right."

"But how did you know that you loved Daddy?"

"Oh, I don't love Daddy. But we get to be on TV every year when they do *The Bachelor-Where is He Now?*"

If that was how it works in the real world, I'd stay out of touch with reality. I prefer my own little world. Squabbles are kept private. Husbands hot tub with their own wives. No one gets voted out of the house and no one has to eat bugs or rodents.

I think reality TV is an oxymoron anyway. It's television, plain and simple. But would I want to marry a millionaire? No, but if my hubby turns out to be one, that'd be great. Just keep the cameras away.

Go To War? Let's Take A Poll

(February, 2003)

છે૦૯

By the time these words hit print, war could be a reality. I have not forgotten we're in the middle of the war against terrorism, but Afghanistan has faded to the background of my mind. We didn't ferret out Osama, so the angle has shifted. The new issue is the "possible" war against Iraq.

I'm ashamed to admit I have my head in the sand. I don't watch television news and only read the headlines of the daily paper. I'm not in denial. I operate on a need to know basis.

My brain and my heart can only handle so much. The state of the world saddens me, and I don't like uncertainty. I want hard answers, decisions, and an end. I'm not naïve enough to believe that there is an end, but that's what I want.

I take the only action I can. I participate in online polls. Computer polls are meaningless, of course, but fascinating. The strategy of our country is not in the hands of people who spend too much time online. Or is it?

"Colin Powell, what do you think?"

"Well, Mr. President, 44% of Americans believe war with Iraq will start in late February; 20% predict March; 18% say early February; and 5% say sometime after March. And get this, 13% maintain we won't go to war. Poor sweet souls, God love 'em."

"How many people were polled?"

"Results were gathered from 250,000 respondents."

"Not enough. We need at least 500,000 opinions before making a decision. Looks like those who bet on early February are going to be wrong. Give the American people what they want – late February it is."

Foreign policy based on "ask the audience" polls seems very American. Another America Online question: "Do you fear war with Iraq would prompt terrorism?" A whopping 1.3 million people responded, with 65% saying yes. We've learned the hard way that terrorism happens without any prompt.

Remember the good old days when online voting was for the worst dressed celebrity? Now the question posed is: "Who is the biggest evil?" I wanted the choices to be comic book villains. The big winner was Osama bin Laden with 40%; Saddam Hussein and Kim Jong II tied with 30% each.

Before September 11, 2001, I'd never heard of Osama. Until this poll, I wasn't sure of the name of the head "bad guy" of North Korea. Now I know.

After entering a response to the poll question, links are given for more information. Topics include Three Possible Attack Strategies, US Weapons and How They Work, and Bases of US Forces. The fate of our country is not in the hands of people who spend too much time online. Or is it?

Why Can't I Just Be Like Everybody Else?

(February, 2003)

ক৵৶

Every one of us has probably felt that desire at some point in our life. We all vacillate between the need to fit in and the wish to stand out. It's human nature.

This night it was my godson, Tanner, voicing the question, "Why can't I just be like everybody else?" He meant it only as a passing complaint. He was tired of injections, pills, and doctors. He was just plain tired.

Tanner is eleven and lives in Iowa. I vividly remember holding him as an infant, his sleeping baby body snuggled into a tiny ball. I instantly loved him. He was born a regulation seven-pounder, but as he aged, his growth didn't keep regulation pace.

The baby magazines say not to compare children, each grows in his own time. Tanner didn't cut teeth and didn't outgrow his shoes. His hair stayed baby fine, even at age two. Well-baby check-ups stated all was well, but Mama and Daddy took Tanner to Iowa City doctors. Tests revealed his pituitary gland was not producing human growth hormone. Tanner needed daily growth hormone injections.

Tanner's folks learned to mix the drug and administer the shot (they call it the "zapper") on alternating thighs each night. A chart on the fridge reminds which leg gets zapped. What was new and a little scary has now become as routine as taking a daily vitamin.

Tanner has been zapping for eight years. New tests recently discovered that his adrenal gland is not producing cortisol, something our bodies need to live, not just grow. Tanner's body isn't making it for him, so he has to take pills three times a day for the rest of his life.

If he gets sick, Tanner will need an instant mega-dose of this hormone. This injection makes the zapper seem like a mosquito bite. He'll need large quantities immediately in the event of an accident or surgery. The boy has to wear a medic alert tag at all times. It's something new and a little scary.

This night, Tanner was tired and just wanted to go to sleep. He wanted to be like other kids who went to bed without shots and pills. At that moment, I'm sure his parents wished that he didn't need a zapper or a pill, but never would they wish he was just like everybody else.

Sure, he is like other kids. He plays basketball with his friends; he fights with his sister; and like to play video games for hours on end. But what do we truly love about other people? The qualities that set them apart.

Tanner is patient, kind, and loving. He knows how to work hard because many things have come hard for him. He knows that life isn't always easy, and he perseveres. He has an amazing work ethic for a young boy. He is sweet and a peacemaker. Tanner has a compassionate soul and that's what this world needs. I wish many things for my godson, but never do I wish for him to be just like everybody else.

PMS – Don't Ever Question It

(April, 2003)

What if there is no PMS and this is really my personality? I read that somewhere and I liked it. I can be crabby any old time, with or without hormones running amok, but there are days that go beyond crabby. PMS is real. It is very real.

Those three letters are scarier to men than the three little words, "I love you." How do I know? All the men stopped reading this column. That's okay. We can girl-talk now. We need to chat occasionally without the guys around. It's good for our mental health. That's what PMS is about – Preserving Mental Sanity.

PMS is code for Stay Away From Me Because I Could Rip Your Head Off With My Bare Hands. I love my husband and my children, but they can be extremely irritating. Most days I deal with their annoying habits with a smile and a hug because I live my life to please my family. But then the moment strikes when I've had enough.

I'm sick and tired of all the socks, balls, and papers that have been lying around the house for a month. I'm sick and tired of the bickering. I'm sick and tired of all the demands on my time and me. If I reach my breaking point at the same time each month, it may be coincidence.

Or it may be Mother Nature's way of letting me express myself freely and get my house in order. "Pick it up! NOW!" One word commands work best around my house. "Shoes!" "Coats!" "Books!" I can envision my boys mimicking me in the future. I maintain that I'm not doing my job as a mother if they don't have stories about me.

I do a shaking gesture in the air with my fists tightly clenched and my jaw locked as I growl. I want to have their little heads in my grasp and shake them silly, but I just shake the air. It gets the frustration out and I don't get locked away. It also gives my sons another good "make fun of Mom" thing.

PMS was originally called BMT, Bring Me Tissues. It was too easily confused with the ever popular BLT sandwich, so the name didn't stick. There are times when I enjoy a good cry. A moving story or movie can evoke the tears. Then there are times when anything and everything can bring on the tears. BMT because it's PMS and I want a BLT because I feel FAT.

I cry because my clothes don't fit. I cry because I ate all the mini chocolate donuts. I don't cry because I ate them all; I cry because I want more and the store closed at 9:00. I cry because I want to beat up somebody. I cry because no one understands.

So I need to be alone. It's good to be alone sometimes. That's another benefit of PMS. No one wants to be around me anyway so Provide Me Solitude. Provide Me Sweets. Provide Me Whatever I Want. What if there is no PMS? Don't ever question it. PMS is real. It is very real.

Words Of Son Written On Mom's Heart

(April, 2003)

ॐॐ

"Hit the moon, Daddy." Those words are written across my heart. I can picture that evening as if it were yesterday, but it was years ago. My boys were knee-high to me then, and we were in the yard of our first house. Blue twilight sky, air still warm, no breeze at all. Daddy was throwing a ball high up into the air to amuse the boys.

"Higher, Daddy, higher!" An act so simple, yet so mesmerizing. Over and over, Daddy threw the ball straight up and straight down it landed in his glove. "Hit the moon, Daddy." My younger son spoke those words with such conviction. With every ounce of his little being, he believed his daddy could throw the ball high enough to hit the big moon hanging in the cloudless sky.

My baby is celebrating his ninth birthday this week and now knows that his dad can't throw a ball that far. My sons are getting so big that some days I think they can throw a ball that high. They're growing up, but still have unwavering confidence in their dad. They've figured out Daddy isn't perfect, but Dad is still first choice with them.

The Man of the Place enjoyed the times when the boys were small, but eagerly anticipated when they'd be old enough to play sports. I didn't want to rush it; I knew that time would come soon enough. And it did. Our days are now fun and exciting, but the sweet and innocent part is fading away.

There are moments. My boys made a flower garden for me. My older son, of his own free will, is spending his own money, a large chunk of it, on a birthday gift for his brother. The boys still like to play games with Mom and Dad. I know the innocence can't last, but maybe the sweet part can. I hope trust in their parents is something my boys will always have.

As they hit the teen years, they'll probably reach a point where they think Dad and I know nothing. It's all a part of growing up. While this growing up is happening, we parents must honor the trust our kids have placed in us. Giving them a good foundation can be exhausting, but it's necessary. We have to kick them out into world ready to go it alone. We have to be ready for that too.

I don't want to rush it. I know that time will come soon enough. That night in the moon glow is a sweet memory for me. My two little toddlers who wrapped themselves around my legs are now two big boys who try to wrap me around their little fingers. They're a lot taller now, and have big feet, but they're my babies.

Right now, when I close my eyes, I can still hear a little voice excitedly shout, "Hit the moon, Daddy."

I'm A Gum Junkie

(October, 2003)

෨ඦ

"Nine out of ten dentists surveyed recommended sugarless gum for their patients who chewed gum." (The tenth dentist recommended sucking on sugar cubes.) My fuzzy memory recalls a TV announcer making that statement in a serious TV voice. The same voice asked a little girl in a ball cap, chomping her gum like a cow chewing its cud, about "chewing a lot of gum out there." She replied: "Trident sugarless gum. It's the only gum my mom lets me chew."

That was before Bubble Yum, BubbleTape, and Bubbalicious. Kids today have a myriad of choices. I loved Fruit Stripes, even though the flavor lasted all of three seconds, and Bazooka, but chewing it gave me a headache.

I recently bought some Fruit Stripes. The miracles of modern science have not been wasted on this gum. The flavor still only lasts three seconds. My kids love all the various bubble gums, but the pieces are huge. I chew half a chunk and my jaw tires out in ten minutes.

Now that I'm the mom, guess what I chew? Yep. Trident sugarless gum. Trident White. It's new, sugar free,

66

and supposed to whiten my teeth. I haven't noticed my teeth getting whiter and I should because I can't get enough of this gum. I can't stop chewing it. I could skip meals because I don't want to take my gum out. I'm buying it up in bulk, and it's the only thing on my Christmas list.

I'm addicted. I'm a gum junkie.

The package says the gum contains something called Recaldent and states it is milk derived. I never drink milk, but I can't go an hour without this gum. I think Recaldent is the habit-forming ingredient. Something in there is.

The back label states: "Phenylketonurics: contains phenylalanine." That could mean: "Warning. This gum is highly addictive." Therefore, the manufacturer couldn't be sued if they said it was addictive right on the package. I'm sure the ingredient isn't harmful to me. It only causes me to keep buying more gum. Genius.

My research discovered that the whitening product is "proprietary (meaning secret) surfactant (meaning surface agent) technology (meaning the average gum chewing mom wouldn't understand it). Trident states subjects chewed two pieces four times a day for 20 minutes to diminish "extrinsic stains."

The whitening claim is probably just propaganda. Anyone who chews that much gum is producing enough saliva to wash away minor stains. I better not have stains on my teeth; I'm chewing my quota way longer than 20 minutes.

It's just my hunch that this gum is addictive. I have no proof. Before Geraldo or *Dateline* can do an investigative report and come up with the hard evidence, I have a plan. I don't want to put the gum makers out of business. I'm hooked and would suffer severe withdrawal if I had to go without this gum. I will threaten the company with an expose revealing their secret proprietary recipe. In return for my silence, they will give me a lifetime supply of Trident White.

And if that doesn't work, I'm off to the store to buy more gum.

Girl-Power Music Over The Years

(November, 2003)

৵৽৻

Karen Carpenter may be rolling over in her grave. I've betrayed her. I did something that I swore to myself I would never do. I bought a Shania Twain CD.

Karen and moody brother Richard were the 70's sensation, The Carpenters. Brooding and sad were many of their songs, but I loved them. "Rainy days and Mondays always get me down." "We go on hurting each other." "I'll say good bye to love; no one ever cared if I should live or die." Oh, the drama.

In high school, I switched Karen for Pat Benatar. Teenage girls need a tough cookie role model; a spike in the hair and a spike in attitude. Pat was music to play while cruising. She could really belt it out. Great stuff for lip sync.

Before the Carpenters could fade away into oblivion or become a lounge act on the has-been circuit, Karen Carpenter died at the age of 33. It was 1983, my freshman year in college. I remember because a fellow student wore a black arm band for an entire week. It was also the same year I went to my first Pat Benatar concert.

Twenty years later, I am not a brooding adolescent or a chick with spunk. When Shania hit the scene in the 90's, I was in maternal mode, playing nursery rhymes on CD. I didn't want to see her flat stomach or hear her songs. *Sing Along with Mickey Mouse* met my needs.

Here we are in the new millennium and my fave CD is Shania's *Up!* After being anti-Shania all these years, it's hard to publicly confess that I like her music. I had vowed to never add my money to her millions, and I didn't want to perpetuate the myth that Shania can sing.

I now admit that she does have talent, although I don't think she belongs with VH-1 Divas, the gals who really have the pipes. We live in a video age and a good voice is not the sole key to success. If Shania were fat and ugly, we would not know her name.

Her other saving grace is that she writes catchy little songs. Shania does write them so I give credit where credit is due. Her songs have upbeat, playful lyrics, toe-tapping tunes, and an underlying current of female empowerment. She's not just a pretty face. That is also her next single.

I like her stuff. Shania is a mom now too, and still looks great in those thigh high boots. More power to her. I've jumped on the girl-power bandwagon because her songs give women a little confidence boost and are fun to sing along with while shuttling kids around town.

My CD player is a good example of how different women can all find common ground while each do their own thing. I need different songs for different moods. Karen, Pat, and Shania are all there for me. They co-exist peacefully, and respect each other. That's real girl power. Or as Shania would say, "Man! I feel like a woman!" I think Karen would agree.

The Message Is: "Look At My Butt"

(November, 2003)

◈◈◈

They're everywhere. I thought it was a passing fad, but this fashion statement is sticking around. Teenage girls wear sweat pants with words emblazoned across the rear end. No matter the word, "Cute," "UCLA," or "Pinch Me," the real message is "look at my butt."

I shake my head with envy. Do it while you can, girls.

My fashion consultants, my boys, tell me I could wear sweats like that. "BIG" or "WIDE LOAD" tickle their fancy. They think "Danger: Hazardous Gas" would be hilarious. I think "Made You Look" would be clever.

As women age, more words fit on the gluteus maximus. The classic, "Does this make my butt look fat?" could be popular. Depending upon my mood, I'd wear "Yeah, baby, I still got it," or "Thanks! No one has checked out my butt since 8th grade."

Mother-daughter sweats could become a trend. Daughter butt: CHEER. Mom butt: "Would you believe this butt used to fit into a cheerleader skirt?" Mess with minds by stating "Objects in sweat pants are smaller than they appear." Just for fun, print in vertical letters: Cheek 2 Cheek.

Certain communities are banning billboards so I predict derriere advertising will be common in the future. Young girls can make bucks renting their rumps to Nike with a big swoosh on the tush. Your daughter could earn cash for college by plastering Heineken on her heinie. The Army could attract more recruits with "Be all you can be" brandished on All-American behinds.

It's bumper stickers, plain and simple. My more mature bumper could work for Jell-o.™ See it wiggle; see it jiggle. Plastic surgeons could drum up business for lipo suction: 1-800-SUCK-FAT. Fitness clubs could do a dual campaign. Tight buns wear "Gold's Gym." Doughy buns wear "Gold's Gym? Is that next to the donut shop?" Sort of the opposite of the old public service ad, "this is your brain/this is your brain on drugs." This is your butt at Gold's; this is your butt if you don't go to Gold's.

Certain songwriters think bigger is better regarding the backside. Their lyrics could result in size appropriate butt wear slogans. Small: "Bootylicious." Medium: "I like big butts, and I cannot lie." Large: "Fat bottom girls, you make the rockin' world go round."

"If you don't use it, you lose it" does not apply to butts. If you don't use it, you get a whole lot more of it. Sit on it and it will grow. My butt used to be a separate entity from my legs. Over time, they have merged into a new flesh I call the "bleg," the combined area of drooping butt into upper leg.

I need a butt bra to lift and separate my butt from my leg, giving me back the fanny of my youth. Bleg be gone. Then I'll wear words across the seat of my pants: "The butt stops here."

Unpacking Memories

(June, 2004)

⊱⊰

We are in the latest house and guess what happens when you unpack? You find things long forgotten, and you uncover memories.

I didn't unearth my Andy Gibb necklace, but I found photos of the concert. It's amazing how a single glance at those pictures instantly transported me to the Wisconsin State Fair, all the way back to when I was in 8th grade. With one look, a smile and a sigh, I was there in that stadium, screaming and swooning with my friend Jeannie.

Unpacking takes a long time when you unpack memories. I flipped through photo albums of trips to Disney World when the boys were younger. Andrew was two, and Tyler was three, the first time we visited the Magic Kingdom. We saw every princess, character, and villain, except for Cinderella.

Cinderella was playing hard to get, and she was the one my baby wanted to see. Our last night there, I tucked him into bed and he pulled my face down right against his. "Mommy, I need to see Cinderella." I will never know why he had a thing for the shoeless girl, but I was determined my son would meet Cinderella.

We had spent time in the autograph lines and my boys had gotten braver each day, but it was very unlike my little boy to plant a sweet kiss on Cinderella's cheek the next morning when she was indeed holding court in her castle. If he ends up a hopeless romantic, it started when he was two.

I bought myself a turntable with this move, so I finally got to unpack my albums. Memories come with a soundtrack. A new needle on an old vinyl record is the closest thing to heaven on earth. I dusted off Scandal's "Goodbye To You," and I was back in time, in a sweaty dorm room dance party. Our new house is very private so I can crank my tunes and dance in my kitchen with no neighborhood witnesses. Billy Idol's "Dancing With Myself" is appropriate.

It may be slow going, but unpacking is a pastime unto itself. Sure, dishes get put in the cupboards, clothes go into the closets, and the garage gets organized so we can park the cars. That stuff is just stuff. It finds a place and gets put away. The real stuff of life is the little things, the memories. Now that I have unpacked them, I don't want to stash them away.

I need to find a place for them, not out of sight and out of mind. I want to put a little something here and there, in plain sight, to be memory triggers for me. That is exactly what a new place needs, reminders of the places we have been before.

And while I am unpacking, I think I'll play some Bob Seger. He said it best. These are the memories that make me a wealthy soul.

Feed The World

(July, 2004)

ಱಲ

The date was July 13, 1985. The place was Wembley Stadium, London. The event was Live Aid. I was there. I was a part of rock-and-roll history, baby. Well, okay, not an integral part, but I was there in the crowd of thousands who came for a once-in-a-lifetime concert thrill and who came to save lives.

The guy who formed Band Aid and put on this "really big show" was Bob Geldof of the UK band, Boomtown Rats. I knew their 1979 song, "I Don't Like Mondays," about a schoolgirl who brought a gun to the school yard and shot her classmates and a teacher. When asked why, she replied, "I don't like Mondays." The news item stuck in Bob's head, and he wrote a song.

In October 1984, Geldof watched a news report of the Ethiopian famine. The pictures horrified him; the images stuck in his head. He wrote a song. He gathered over 40 pop stars and in November of that year, they recorded "Feed the World/Do They Know It's Christmas." This one little record sold worldwide and raised eight million pounds (that's a lot of British bucks) to feed starving people.

The spectacular success of the record kept millions of people alive, but Geldof said, "Now we must give them a life." In order to raise money for long term development projects, the idea of a concert was born. Not just any concert, a concert and telethon performed on two continents linked by satellite, and televised around the world. Across time zones, across oceans, hundreds of people joined in the vision and produced "the greatest rock show ever."

Geldof thought it important to make a "grand gesture" to get the attention of governments. He was appalled that millions in Africa were starving while the European Economic Commission had just spent 265 million pounds to destroy two million tons of fruit and vegetables. "In a world of surplus, death by starvation is the most preposterous and evil death of all."

Even more extraordinary than coordinating over sixty artists (who all donated their time), the attendance of 72,000 at Wembley and over 100,000 in Philadelphia, and the millions of dollars raised, was that it all started with one guy who saw a news report, and thought, "I gotta do something." And he did.

How many of us have thought that, or do we wait for someone else to "do something"? Sometimes we think what we do won't matter. It does. It starts with one person, one idea. Bob Geldof was just a guy from a punk rock band. Because he did something, others did too. If Bob had done nothing, I would not have had the concert experience of my life. (Thanks, Bob.) If Bob had done nothing, millions more in Ethiopia would have died.

He was just a guy, moved to write a song, not knowing that "Feed the World" would become his life's mission. When something hits you in the heart, you have choice. Do nothing. Do something. It's your choice.

Life Begins At 40

(September, 2004)

৵৽

I made a conscious decision to not freak out about turning forty. In fact, I decided to celebrate 40 Days of Turning 40. My celebration was going well until the morning of the day before my birthday. I looked in the mirror and it hit me: This is my last day as a 30-something. I loved being a 30-something. I wasn't ready for it to be over, but I guess it is always best to leave the party while you're still having fun.

The Man of the Place hugged me tight and promised that he'd still love me tomorrow when I was officially old. He endured my drama queen questions. "Has my chin always had this dangling turkey skin?" "What is this loose jiggly stuff under my bicep?" "Look at the bulging veins on my hands! Have they always looked like this?" Skin-firming lotion suddenly became number one on my birthday list.

I took a cake into work this birthday eve day. Awaiting me on my desk was an "Oh No, the Big Four-Oh!" hat, adorned with shiny silver fringe and Tootsie Pops. It's hard to be down in the dumps when wearing a Tootsie Pop hat. It was quite the conversation piece and a nice distraction to get me through my final day as a 30-something. The 40 days of turning 40 were over. Forty was staring me down.

My colleagues reassured me that life at 40 was wonderful. One gal said her forties were her best decade and she wished she could live those years over and over again. All of my esteemed and very wise co-workers adamantly agreed that forty is fabulous and freeing.

Freedom from worrying about what others think. Freedom from the constant demands of little ones. (If you are just starting a family at 40, you're not free just yet.) Freedom to express myself in my own way. A Tootsie Pop hat suits me. Freedom is a very thoughtful birthday gift.

I'm forty now. I'm okay. I can assume that I will live to a ripe old age, but one can never be sure. Instead of bemoaning the fact that I'm aging, I'll celebrate the fact that I'm living. Every year I'll get wiser and pass on freeing thoughts to others in their moment of doubt.

My mid-life crisis was a fleeting moment. I didn't run off with a younger man or buy a convertible. The Man of the Place is a younger man, so maybe I'll rent a convertible for the weekend. Ah, freedom! Happy Birthday to me.

It's Not Easy Being Cruella DeVil

(October, 2004)

ھوجء

I am Cruella DeVil. The only difference is that Cruella would do anything to obtain puppy fur and I would do anything to be rid of it. I won't hire bumbling goons to kidnap my dog, but I'm tempted. I hate dog hair that much.

Seasonal shedding is a bald-face lie told by dog sellers. It is only something snakes do. As sure as our dog is breathing, she is shedding. With every exhale, short little black hairs eject themselves from her body and dive bomb into our carpet, clothing, and furniture. Nothing is safe, even the walls.

Her hairs are the stealthiest stuff I've ever known. They are like little needles and have to be pulled out one by one from the carpet. It's a wonder that our dog is not bald. I've pleaded with my husband to shave her, but he refuses. He says a Black Lab would get a Poodle complex if we shaved her. Poodles don't shed so I say it's worth a try.

The vet says to brush her every day and that would help control the shed. I barely manage to brush my own hair every day. Hmmm, come to think of it, I shed a lot too.

Glenn Close may have fared well being Cruella, but not me. My family rolls their eyes and says, "Mom is ranting about dog hair again." They, being of the male species, don't see the hair nor does it concern them. Why does it bother me so? I wish I knew. I was raised in a pet-free environment which could be part of the reason. It's all in what you're used to.

I could have lived out my life perfectly happy without ever having a pet (I hear the gasps out there. I told you, I'm Cruella DeVil.) The Man of the Place and the little men begged for a dog, so I gave in. That was almost six years ago. I should have adjusted by now. I should not be freaked by a dog hair in the fridge or in an ice cube, but it grosses me out.

The new house layout has banished the dog from the kitchen, so those incidents no longer happen. (Note to dinner guests, you still might want to double check your drink.) Tonight my rampage started when I poured fabric softener into the washing machine and all I saw was black hair.

"Get the shop vac and vacuum the dog!" I screamed. I cycled the washer sans clothes and started again. The Man of the Place asked me what I was doing. "Trying to clean our clothes, not distribute wet dog hair all over them!"

"In that mood again, huh?" he smirked.

The mood will pass, but it never completely goes away. Just like the dog hair.

I'll vacuum out the washer and dryer, the furniture, and the van, and the dog. She likes it. I wish I didn't hate dog hair. It bothers me that it bothers me. I hate dog hair, and I hate the fact that I do. It ain't easy being Cruella DeVil.

A Day To Be Thankful

(November, 2004)

♥

Today is a day to be thankful. Do you go around the table and have everyone say what they are thankful for? Do you make fun of people who do?

I'm thankful for Caffeine Free Coca-Cola. I'm thankful for all cola products, automatic ice makers, and pretty glassware. I'm thankful for dishwashers, refrigerators, and electric mixers. I'm thankful for butter and *I Can't Believe It's Not Butter.* I'm thankful for fresh bread.

I'm thankful for hot showers. I'm thankful for sunshine, lollipops, and rainbows. I'm thankful for pilgrims, Indians, and pirates (okay, just Johnny Depp). I'm thankful for television, radio, and movie theaters with floors that aren't sticky. I'm thankful for popcorn.

I'm thankful for a van with heated seats. I'm thankful for covered bridges, scenic byways, and Mapquest. I'm thankful for bottled water, Laffy Taffy, and gum. I'm thankful gas stations always have gas. I'm thankful for pay at the pump. I'm thankful for clean restrooms.

I'm thankful for Winnie the Pooh. I'm thankful for laptop computers, the internet, and wireless technology. I'm thankful for mascara, hair spray, and glitter nail polish. I'm thankful for rainy days and Mondays when Karen Carpenter sings. I'm thankful for small towns, big cities, and rolling country landscapes. I'm thankful for Tigger too.

I'm thankful for second chances. I'm thankful for sight, hearing, and the sense of touch. I'm thankful for old friends, new friends, and friends I don't know yet. I'm thankful for imagination, day dreams, and wishes come true. I'm thankful for forgiveness.

I'm thankful for anticipation. I'm thankful for vacations, work, and the weekends. I'm thankful for clean sheets, new socks, and old sweats. I'm thankful for jammies, blankies, and good books. I'm thankful for songwriters, heartache, and happy endings. I'm thankful for disappointment.

I'm thankful for Life – the cereal and the one God gave me. I'm thankful for a husband who loves me and at times even adores me. I'm thankful for two amazing sons. I'm thankful for those folks we call family. I'm thankful for Vick's Vapor Rub.

I'm thankful for peanut butter. I'm thankful for back scratchers, bug zappers, and Yahtzee. I'm thankful for redneck jokes, old boyfriends, and Elvis. I'm thankful for

Little House on the Prairie, Walt Disney, and my backyard. I'm thankful for Barry Manilow.

I'm thankful for dentists. I'm thankful for doctors, lawyers, and bankers. I'm thankful for candles, sparklers, and fireworks. I'm thankful for things that make me laugh, things that make me cry, and things that make me think. I'm thankful for things that glow in the dark.

I'm thankful to live in the USA. I'm thankful for comfy couches, sleeper sofas, and pillow top mattresses. I'm thankful for reading, writing, and arithmetic. I'm thankful for nice neighbors. I'm thankful that the list never ends. Today is a day to be thankful and I'm thankful for you.

Home Sweet Home

(March, 2005)

&oe&

My office is currently the kitchen table. Right now my younger son is at the opposite end of the table building a bridge out of Styrofoam peanuts. (They stick together with water. Who knew?)

My older son is giving his trombone a bath in my tub. Their retainers are soaking in denture cleaner on the kitchen counter. Also on the counter are leftover Valentine chocolates, a candy bag from a birthday party, three forgotten heart-shaped cookies, a brown banana, and a freshly opened package of Oreos.™ Candy wrappers and crumbs complete the display. It's called Home Sweet Home for a reason.

Within my eyeshot, there are four half-full water glasses. Every time they're thirsty, my boys grab a new glass from the cupboard without recalling that they just did so half an hour ago. My sons like their water on the rocks with a twist (a bendy straw). I prefer my water carbonated with caramel color, high fructose corn syrup, and caffeine. I drink from a goblet. (The counter is also littered with two goblets. Don't tell my boys.)

From my perch here at the end of the table, I can see into the living room where the Man of the Place is playing Pac-Man on the TV. The game was a Christmas gift to the boys, but Dad has taken it over. He reached the level of three keys; from the hootin' and hollerin', I guess that's good. A dot-munching yellow circle being chased around a maze by Inky, Blinky, and Speedy has stood the test of time, and now gives an old married guy stress relief. Life is kooky.

The dog is whining so I leave the table to investigate. She had her waffle this morning, her regular food, treats, and a rawhide bone. She is on point staring at her food bin. Her yip distinctly says, "You leave me home alone all day everyday. I know you feel guilty so if I look deep into your eyes, you'll give me more treats." Oh Starburst, would that I could, but the vet says you need to lose ten pounds and he doesn't even know about the waffles.

As I throw her ball around the family room and play tug, she gives up on me and goes to her boys for some loving. On my way back to the kitchen, I trip over basketballs (two regulation size and three Nerf), drum sticks (the broken duct-taped ones and the new ones), a percussion practice pad, and a guitar amp. Some days I'd yell to pick up the stuff. Tonight it doesn't bother me. Life is cluttered.

I'm trying to live in the moment. Enjoy more. Stress less. We have everything we need, and much of what we want. We are healthy. Most days we like being together. Sometimes my big boys still call me "mama" and it melts my heart. Life is kooky. Life is cluttered. Life is sweet.

The Man of the Place has put down the Pac-Man joystick and is folding a load of laundry while I write. Life doesn't get any better than that. Home Sweet Home, it certainly is.

Do Blondes Really Have More Fun?

(April, 2005)

It's not a lie. I'd always tried to convince myself that it was hogwash, but it's true. Blondes have more fun. Somewhere deep inside of me, I feared it may be true, but I never allowed myself to admit it out loud. Being a brunette, I held onto the strongest thing we women have – denial.

One of my best friends in high school had beautiful blonde Farrah hair. Jeannie got attention. I got frizzies. My brown hair never behaved the way I wished it would. I never behaved the way blonde girls did. I didn't walk into a room expecting heads to turn. I didn't playfully run my fingers through my hair. I didn't toss my head back and laugh the way blondes did.

Blondes have more fun because they have more confidence. Why? Because America loves blondes. Blonde hair and blue eyes is the ideal. The magazines and TV ads prove the U.S. of A. is overpopulated with blondes.

People notice blondes, and it doesn't matter if it's natural or from a box. Do you think Marilyn Monroe was born blonde? Do you think John Kennedy cared? No one was born with her platinum color, but ooh, la, la, we like it. Aging blondes may get gray hairs, but they blend in and aren't noticeable. My gray hairs are a stark contrast to my dark hair, and they boing up like antenna wires.

So I did it. I went blonde. I figured I'm 40 now, what the heck. Girls just want to have fun. I went to the store and bought a box of "I'm worth it" color. I didn't want to be seen in public until I could get used to seeing myself in the mirror without screaming, laughing, or crying. The Man of the Place loves it. My boys hate it.

Blondes do have more fun. The teenage boys at the drive-up window flirt with me. Or maybe I am flirting with them. I wear a little more makeup now and never go anywhere without lipstick. I wear pointy high heels with jeans. There are no men in my office, but the delivery guy now knows me by name. I walk into a room and heads turn. I run my fingers through my Farrah locks. I toss my head back and laugh.

Why am I laughing? Because you fell for it! Gotcha! April Fool's! I am NOT blonde and never will be. No offense to all you beautiful blondes, but I actually like being a brunette. Someone has to stay dark-headed so the blondes will stand out.

I am okay being not-so-noticeable at a party. Too much attention makes me uncomfortable. But do blondes really have more fun? I'll fight you on that one. I have fun every day, and I had fun pulling my April Fool's joke on you. And besides, I would look horrible as a blonde.

Take Your Candle, Light Your World

(May, 2005)

ॐॐ

"Why, what candle-snuffing words, Peter." That wonderfully descriptive phrase (and Johnny Depp's accent) resonated with me long after the movie ended. In *Finding Neverland*, Depp portrays author J.M. Barrie, a famous playwright in a bit of a slump. In the park, he meets a widow and her four young sons. They embark on a summer of playful adventures, creating jungles and crocodiles, pirate ships, and swashbuckling sword fights. Their tales became the play, *Peter Pan*, Barrie's most successful work.

The lad, Peter, was a sensitive soul. He originally disparages silliness, fancy, and imagination, hence Barrie's admonition. Ultimately, Peter discovered that he was a dramatist himself. "Uncle Jim" Barrie gifted Peter a leather bound journal of his own, so he too could record his musings.

Never a fan of *Peter Pan,* I enjoyed the story behind the story, and wondered how often I have uttered candle snuffing words. I don't want to diffuse the imagination in my boys and I don't want to extinguish the flame of inspiration in my friends.

How many times do we unwittingly dampen the spirit of another? We say, "Oh, don't be silly!" Why not? What's wrong with silly? Perhaps even well-intentioned advice is candle snuffing. We tell friends to "play it safe" or "don't be crazy."

A child who constantly hears "Be careful" needs to also hear "You can do it." We may mean well, but instead of encouraging, we create hesitation, timidity, and fear. I'm not endorsing reckless abandon of all reason, but we should give those we love wings to fly, and be careful to not clip those wings.

The phrase "candle snuffer" reminded me of another term that I don't want to be. This story belongs to a former co-worker. Paula and her father were at the grocery store. They saw a man reach into the cooler for a package of cheese. It slipped from his grasp and fell to the floor. Instead of picking it up, he muttered and gave it a forceful kick, sending the cheese skidding across the dirty linoleum tiles.

Paula and her dad exchanged glances, but said nothing. They got to the car in the parking lot to find a grocery cart rammed into the door. Paula's father calmly stated, "I bet it was that cheese kicker." The label "cheese kicker" forever entered their family lexicon. Paula's young son described a schoolmate with a poor attitude as a real cheese kicker. Cheese kickers and candle snuffers start early in life.

I need to pay attention to my words and behavior. We all have moments of grumbling. Sometimes we can chalk it up to a bad day, but I don't want "cheese kicker" or "candle snuffer" to be my legacy. I don't want to be a dream squasher. I want to be a life giver. Musician Chris Rice wrote a song that says something about each of us has a candle in our soul; some are brightly burning, some are dark and cold.

We can lift up or we can put out. We can light or we can snuff. Rice's advice is the best there is: Take your candle, and go light your world.

A Letter To Readers

(June, 2005)

*

People often ask me what I write about each week in my column. "Whatever pops into my head," I reply. My words are basically a letter that I write to you each week. You'll never know how much you mean to me. I hope our friendship is meant to last because soon we will be embarking on a long distance relationship.

The Man of the Place has been assigned to work on a project for Airbus in France. I think that's worth an exclamation point! We'll be moving to Toulouse, in the south of France, for a year or two. Are you thinking champagne wishes and caviar dreams?!

Toulouse is the fourth largest city in France, five hours from Paris by train, and seventy minutes by plane. We'll be less than two hours to the Mediterranean Sea or the Pyrenees mountains. Toulouse is older than Rome, teeming with beauty and history. Oh, there go my goose bumps again! We could spend an entire year just in Toulouse and the surrounding area, and never run out of things to do and see.

When Life Stinks,... Wash the Gym Clothes

Of course, one does not take an international assignment if one does not plan to make the most of the adventure. Our boys are currently 5th and 6th grades, and they're incredibly excited about the trip. We are focusing on all the positive aspects of the trip. We'll go to Paris of course. Rome is on the list. My younger son will have his wish come true to visit Amsterdam and see Anne Frank's hiding place with his own eyes. I get misty just thinking about it.

When we learned that we were going, I pulled out the globe. "Mom, I know my European countries," elder son chastised me. I don't. I need a map. What countries border France? Spain, Germany, Italy, Belgium, Switzerland. Pinch me. This has to be a dream.

There are (honestly, cross my heart, no exaggeration) one million details to tend to before we leave. Our boys will return to their same school here, and they will go to an English speaking school there. My employer has granted me a leave of absence so I have my job when we return. How blessed is that? I'm a little panicky because I have so much to do to turn over the reins to someone else. If my co-workers discover how unorganized I really am, they'll change their minds about letting me come back.

Lucky for me, my side job - my letter writing to you – is emailed each week. The world wide web really is world wide. I'll rely heavily on the cyber connection this coming year. Technology will allow the kids to stay in touch with their buddies and teachers. We plan to make a web page called eppyfamily.com to post photos and blog our journey. The time away will be a learning experience in so many ways.

We're thrilled to have this opportunity. I'll keep you posted. Au revoir!

The Scary, Hairy French Doctor

(July, 2005)

෧෨

Our first encounter with a French doctor was scary. La Republique de Francais requires medical approval for Americans to live in France. The week of our arrival, we spent two hours searching Toulouse for the tiny, back-alley Office des Migrations Internationales.   We had to ring the buzzer to be let in, but it was no place I wanted to be.

A young, pierced gal greeted us (i.e., silently stared at us, snatched our paperwork and walked away). A professional-looking woman (lab coat over her cleavage) took us to a desk at the end of a cramped hallway and asked our names and ages in broken English.   "Healthy?" Yes. Check, check, check, check. "Any operations or problems?" No. Check, check, check, check. "Last medical appointment?" I lied and said last month. "For all?" Yes. "Glasses?" Check, check. She squeezed around us to go ask the doctor if the children needed an x-ray or just the adults. Gulp. I'd read that in France the patient is totally naked for any exam or procedure.

She escorted us into the doctor's office which consisted of a desk, two chairs and a stark exam table. Dread washed over me. The doctor was large and greasy with long, dark, wiry curls exploding from his head and arms. He had yellowed teeth and needed a shave. He wore a tight black shirt and gold chains. All four Eppersons visibly shuddered. "No way is this guy touching me," was the shared thought.

The woman barked, "Anglais!" and left us. The doctor grunted, "Bonjour," and proceeded to talk in French. The only anglais he spoke was to ask, "OK?" We nodded. He continued his conversation with himself, but stamped and signed our paperwork. "Voila." (The most common word in the French language; we say it "vwa-la".) That was it. No exam. No x-rays. The scary, hairy doctor did not see us naked.

A few weeks later, I learned my boys needed a French physical for school. The school uses a female doctor who speaks English. We located her office five minutes past the start of office hours. The reception area was dark with no chairs. There were three doors with three names. We opened the door with Dr. Monique's name and discovered a small waiting room. We were fifth in line. The people sitting muttered bonjour and went back to silence.

Dr. Monique's office door would open and the next person jumped up and dashed in. After an hour and forty-five minutes, our turn came. Dr. Monique was friendly, attractive and not hairy. She had the requisite desk, two chairs, and exam table. She examined the boys and explained they needed a tetanus booster and TB shot. In the US, we test for TB. In France, they immunize against it. My kids will now show a positive result when TB tested in the states, but that's another story. (Repeat after me: Everything in France is different. Everything in France takes longer.)

Doctors in France don't have meds. I received a prescription to buy the shots. Dr. Monique said to come back at 3:00 pm and she would administer the immunizations. We were relieved to have a rendezvous, but bemused to have to find a pharmacy. A young, pierced boy, certainly no chemist, filled my order. We arrived at Dr. Monique's slightly before 3 pm, the start of office hours for the afternoon. About 3:45 she breezed in. (Repeat after me: Everything in France is different. Everything in France takes longer.)

So the other day when I awoke with mal a la gorge (sore throat), I silently screamed, "I don't want to go to the doctor!" I sucked enough cough drops to remove a layer of skin off my tongue, but my throat feels better. I won't have to go to the doctor, but I will have to go to the pharmacy to replenish the cough drops. The pharmacy is the only place to buy over-the-counter meds here. Repeat after me: Everything in France is different.

When in France...

(September, 2005)

෨∘෨

I'm no uncultured, unsophisticated, uncouth American. (Burp.) I know steak tartare is raw burger. I didn't know carpaccio de bouef was paper thin slices of raw beef. I couldn't eat it. The French were the founders of the Clean Plate Club. Not only is it an insult to leave food on your plate, it is practically a crime. I'm lucky the chef didn't haul me away to the guillotine.

The Man of the Place ordered salmon and the waiter asked, "Fresh?" Not knowing the alternative, my hubby said yes. It was served chilled and uncooked. The Man can eat raw food; my boys and I do not. *Magret du canard* (breast of duck) is our new favorite. We've learned to have it cooked *bien cuit*, well done, which would be medium in America.

Not knowing foie gras from Kentucky blue grass, I told my boys to order the hotel specialty, foie gras du canard. My darlings were not happy when cold duck liver pate arrived on their plates. Bless their hearts for trying it, but they declared it "duck spam," and passed it to Dad. They don't care what is considered a delicacy. Escargot is on the menu, but they refuse to eat snails too.

One evening, my husband ordered the plate of cheeses as a starter. Oh the shame. Cheese is eaten after the meal. Another night, I ordered an appetizer for us all. No sharing in France. It was placed before me when they were given their food. When they were done and my appetizer finished, my food was brought out to me. We decided that in the future, everyone gets an appetizer or no one does.

Pizzas are yummy, but each person orders their own and they're huge, and yes, eaten with knife and fork. I have my boys help me clean my plate. The fried egg in the middle still surprises me, but at least I can eat it.

I lack an adventurous palate so I have not sampled ostrich or kangaroo. I enjoy lamb and veal, but no horse. *Steak hache* is chopped steak, but not necessarily beef. *Steak hache de cheval* is horse meat and supposedly delicious, but no way can I eat Trigger. Reading the menu carefully is a French lesson and a wise precaution.

Dining out is a long affair, but we quickly acclimated to two hour meals. Service is prompt, but the waiter doesn't continually come back to the table. If we want something, we ask. Otherwise, we are left alone. It is actually quite nice.

Lunch is only served between noon and two. All companies, and most schools, have a standard two hour lunch break. Most stores, banks and post offices close. The lunch hour is just that, not an errand hour. Once you get used to it, it is divine. When I return to America and want a two hour lunch, I wonder how many employers will accommodate.

Dinner is served at 8 p.m. We were hungry one evening and thought certainly the Pizza Hut would serve anytime. Au contraire. When in France, mealtimes are just that. We're learning. Hopefully we'll never stop. Since we are in our house now, we can eat whenever we eat. It may be only 6 p.m., but I'm hungry. Bon appétit!

It's Good To Have A Crush

(October, 2005)

~~

It's good for a girl to have a crush, even an old, happily-married girl. My current crush is Ewan McGregor. I fell for him in the movie, *Moulin Rouge*, and he still makes my heart go beat-beat-beat. Ewan comes in doll form as Obi-Wan Kenobi, the Star Wars Jedi. My darling divas back home knew I needed a friend in France so they sent me the Ewan doll. They had the good sense to ditch the Star Wars uniform and stitched him a divapink outfit instead. He's stunning.

It's good for a girl to have a companion, especially a strong, silent type in a loud, pink shirt. I took my Ewan for photos around our town of Tournefeuille and he kept me company on trips into Toulouse. I've studied Ewan (the man, not the doll) dancing with Renee Zellweger in the movie *Down with Love*. I bought a red dress very similar to Renee's. Thanks to a diva-in-training, I have a photo with me superimposed as Renee so I'm dancing with Ewan in Renee's red dress. It's the next best thing to being there.

As my birthday approached, I decided the perfect gift would be the real Ewan. I booked a flight to London and tickets for "Guys and Dolls" at the Piccadilly Theatre where Ewan is starring as Sky Masterson. My plan was to have Ewan autograph my picture, my doll's pink shirt, and get a real photo with Ewan and me in my red dress.

Before we left for London (The Man of the Place thought it best he and the boys accompany me), I couldn't find my "Ewan and Me" photo. My children begged me to not bring the Ewan doll to London. It was too cold to wear the little red dress and I learned Ewan no longer gives autographs after the show.

It's good for a girl to have a fantasy life, but also good to not lose grasp on reality. I'll never meet Ewan. That's okay. It's Christian, the fictitious penniless writer, who I fell for. Ewan is an actor, married with two young daughters, who probably would think an Obi-Wan doll in a pink shirt was quite strange.

But because of Ewan we went to London. "Guys and Dolls" was marvelous. We splurged on show tickets for the next night as well and took in the homage to Freddie Mercury and Queen in "We Will Rock You." Guess which musical my sons preferred. We spent the weekend being tourists riding the double-decker red bus. My guys were happy because (drum roll please) they speak English in England. They enjoyed riding the tube and figuring out what line we needed and what stop to get off. We have funny memories (my son does a dead-on impression of the guy who sold us theatre tickets) and it was our introduction to real European hotel rooms.

It's good for a girl to dream. It's good for a girl to have a hubby who indulges her and sons who think their mom is a little odd, but love her anyway. I suggested to The Man of the Place that we go to London every year. He pointed out that flights from Illinois may be a little more expensive than flights from France. Such a realist, that guy. But because of Ewan and The Man of the Place, I had an incredible birthday weekend in one of my favorite places in the world. It's good for a girl to have a crush.

Walking In Their Footsteps, History Has More Meaning

(January, 2006)

ॐ

My children knew about World War II, but since our trip to Normandy, textbook facts now have a tangible reference in their minds. Boys seem to have a proclivity for soldier stories, but touring the D-Day beaches helped them comprehend the reality of the events that unfolded, the staggering loss of life, and the utter devastation of war.

Our first stop was the Normandy American Cemetery. Over 9,300 United States servicemen (and four women) are laid to rest in a 172 acre rectangular plot on a cliff overlooking the sea at Omaha Beach. The rows of white headstones are perfectly aligned, facing America, and aren't all crosses as pictures suggest. The Star of David marks the grave of Jewish soldiers.

I wandered the immaculate lawn and read names. Francis, Robert, Edwin. I touched the grave markers. Did Douglas have a Betty Ann back home who wrote him letters every night? Did Johnny want to own a little patch of land when he returned to Oklahoma? Did Peter suffer or did he die instantly? I felt a mother's pain as I imagined the horror that ended their young lives. They were just boys.

The French government donated this land to the United States. The only stipulation, no money be made off the dead. There's no gift shop selling postcards. The small information office is staffed every day to answer questions and assist visitors in locating graves.

The site also has a small limestone chapel with a marble altar and mosaic ceiling. The inscription reads, "Think not only upon their passing, remember the glory of their spirit." I think how afraid they must've been. Heroes all. One is not brave unless one faces fear.

Instead of gathering their dead in one spot, the British have fifteen cemeteries, choosing to bury the fallen on the fields of battle. Normandy has cemeteries for French, Canadian, and Polish soldiers as well.

There are also more than 58,000 Germans buried in France. We visited one of the five small German cemeteries. The bodies are buried on top of each other with modest brown crosses as markers. Birth dates are not listed if they died under the age of eighteen. Most markers had no birth dates. They were just boys.

The D-Day landings were on five beaches: Utah, Omaha, Gold, Juno and Sword. We walked Utah, Omaha and Point du Hoc where American rangers scaled the cliff and suffered heavy casualties only to discover the guns they were sent to capture had already been moved by the Germans.

We explored bunkers and the scarred landscape of bomb craters. Part of the beach area remains as it was, preserved as a memorial. Part is now the scene of vacation homes and summer frolic. Our tour guide, a young, passionate Frenchman, told of an American veteran who cried watching children play on the beach. Some say the beach should stay sacred land. This vet shed tears of joy, stating life was what he fought for.

My younger son wants more World War II books for his birthday. "I know a lot, but I need to learn more." We watch movies together. "Memphis Belle" tells a bomber squadron's story. "The Longest Day" is D-Day. "Band of Brothers" depicts the true tales of Easy Company.

My sweet eleven-year-old looks at me and says, "I could never do that." The images stay with him. At bedtime, he wants me to tuck him in and read Shel Silverstein poems. He's a sensitive soul not made for war. Who really is? I watch my boys sleep and feel that ache in my heart. They were all just boys.

Becoming Bilingual In France, But Not In French

(February, 2006)

꙰꙰꙰

"Would you like garden peas or mushy peas?" The English Speaking Ladies Group monthly walk ended at noon, and we lunched at a village pub owned by a British bloke. The ladies all ordered fish and chips. Mushy peas resembled baby food. "Yucky peas" would be my description.

I've also walked with AIT – Americans in Toulouse. I was one of two Americans in the group. There was an Australian lady, a Scottish lass, an Irish gal, and the rest all hailed from various parts of England. We speak the same language (well, sort of; I can't understand the Scottish gal), but being American puts me in the minority. To them, the United States is overwhelmingly huge. They know Disney World and Las Vegas. Some may not know where Illinois is ("somewhere in the middle?"), but all know Chicago. What do they know about Chicago? Al Capone.

By keeping company with Brits, my family is acquiring the Queen's English. If something's good, it's brilliant; not good, it's rubbish. They don't say really good, but "well good." I find myself saying "quite" and "a bit." It's quite lovely. Would you like a bit more then? I have a telephone, but I don't call my friend Kathy; I ring her. Posh means fancy and fancy means want. A nappy is a diaper, a bat is a ping pong paddle, and a jumper is a sweater. When asked to bring food to a function, it's a sweet or a savory (a non-sweet). Take the carriageway (highway) and use the car park (parking lot) next to the row of flats (apartments).

Sometimes the words are the same, but the inflection is different. Examples won't work in print, but believe me, my sons are picking up an accent from their mates as well as expanding their vocabulary. My boys now claim to be bilingual - American English and British English.

Hallway is corridor. Pencil eraser is rubber. Cookies are biscuits and potato chips are crisps. Four-thirty is half past four. My guys spell words differently to please their teachers: colour, organisation, maths. A study list of commonly confused words included sauce and source, which we generally don't confuse in the states. The British word for homey (as in cozy) is homely, so that could cause a misunderstanding.

Over autumn break, a British boy was going to Houston. My son commented that Houston was in the World

Series. The lad looked at him strangely and said, "No, Houston is in Texas." Baseball and basketball aren't popular here. Soccer is played during lunch break, but it's called football. The game we call football is always "American football."

The British are flocking to the south of France. 250,000 I recently read. They prefer the climate, the food, the pace of life, and the space. The U.K. and France each have a population of 60 million, but France has three times the land.   Many Brits are here on temporary assignment as we are, but just as many have moved here permanently. It's possible to drive to England using the ferry or Channel Tunnel and flights to London are less than two hours and cheap. It makes popping back home to see Mum as easy as steak and ale pie.

I'm slowly becoming bilingual too. Jelly means gelatin. Bin it means to throw it away. Pudding is any dessert. The garden is not flowers or vegetables, it's just the yard. When my friend said her husband needed to lose a stone, she didn't mean a kidney stone. A stone is about fourteen pounds. I'm not daft, I can figure out the lingo. So now I'll get off my bum, grab my rucksack and go queue at the post. Cheerio.

An American in Paris

(March 2006)

బా౼

Americans are infatuated with Paris. I recently took two visiting U.S. gals to gay Pah-ree. The five and a half hour drive on the auto route was easy. The thirty minutes driving in Paris had me sweaty. There's no such thing as staying in your lane as there are no lanes. I used to think Chicago driving was hairy. At least in Chicago, there are rules. After skillful navigation on my part (okay, pure luck) and thanks to two maps, my co-pilots, and the GPS, we arrived at the Hotel de la Tulipe.

The hotel was within walking distance to everywhere (almost) and near the Metro. I was the tour guide. "Look at that. It's old. Look at that. It's pretty."

We were close to Les Invalides with its beautiful gold dome and grassy park area, and Pont Alexandre III, the ornate bridge with gold gilded statues. Crossing this bridge takes you to Place de la Concorde where Louis XVI, Marie-Antoinette, and a lot of other people, were beheaded. It's a lovely setting with fabulous fountains and an Egyptian obelisk marking the spot. "Look at that. It's a tall, pointy thing. A guillotine used to sit here."

It's a given that Americans want to go up the Eiffel Tower. Gustave Eiffel built an impressively tall metal structure (no Leaning Tower of Pisa here). Tourists are packed into an elevator up to the second level viewing area. Another elevator has to be boarded for the aerial view at the top.

Perfect timing, we saw it in daylight and then night fell quickly. The City of Lights glows in the dark. Crossing the bridge over the River Seine, we walked in the chilly night to the Trocadero to snap photos with the twinkling tower in the background.

What do cold Americans do on their first evening in Paris? Go to the English-speaking Hard Rock Café for Margarita Popsicles, of course. We spent the next whirlwind days hitting the "must-see" sights. I warned Le Louvre is huge and Mona Lisa très petite. Seeing was believing. Notre Dame impressed them. Smoky French lunches with five dollar Cokes surprised them. They should have ordered wine like their tour guide. Souvenir shopping was fun and relaxing with no kids and husbands in tow (or maybe it was because of the wine).

I dragged them through the Opera House although neither had seen the Phantom, on stage or film. I dragged them to Moulin Rouge, though neither had seen that movie. I dragged them to the huge and mazelike Père Lachaise cemetery to find Jim Morrison's grave, though neither was a fan of The Doors. We got shushed in the Sacré-Couer Basilica. "It's not that old, but it's pretty." We rode the funicular because "It's fun to ride a funicular" and we were too tired to climb all those stairs.

We shopped Galeries Lafayette with the gorgeous stained glass dome and took in the rooftop view of old Parree. (Proper pronunciation requires a bit of phlegm.) We strolled the Champs-Elysées. We witnessed a guy skid off his motorbike at the Arc de Triomphe. We wandered designer stores pretending we could afford a key chain. We watched a TV crew do interviews on the sidewalk. We went to a late movie (in English with French subtitles) and had the choice of sugar or salt on our popcorn. We walked back to the hotel after midnight in moonlit Paris. It was an express tour, but was expressly enjoyable.

Americans are smitten with Paris. The flowers, the fashion, the architecture, the art, the food, the wine, the history, the chocolate, the French, the tourists, it's all there. Listen to your tour guide. "Look at that. It's pretty."

Nine Month Check-Up

(April, 2006)

&&

Time for a nine month check-up. Can I speak French? Nope. I can order a meal and pay the bill. I'm able to say I speak and understand only a little bit. I can ask them to please talk slower. I can tell the salesgirl that these shoes are too small. I've learned my shoe size is 40.

I may not speak French, but I can look French, right down to my matching bra and panties. It's basic survival. If I were in a car accident, the paramedics would immediately know I wasn't French if they saw boring cotton underwear. I don't want to be left for dead on the side of the road so pretty lingerie is now daily attire. Matching sets are all that's sold here and some of those paramedics are really cute.

What seemed odd when we first arrived is now normal. When out for a walk, if I pass someone on the sidewalk, I don't make eye contact. I don't say hello. That is so American. The French way of friendliness is letting each other be. Greeting a stranger is a sign of senility. I have, however, smiled at dimple-faced babies. Their mothers have replied a genial "bonjour" so there are no absolutes.

The washing machine cycle that takes two hours and nineteen minutes now seems normal. Emptying the water tray after every dryer load seems normal. Adding salt to the dishwasher seems normal. Liter size milk bottles in a sixty centimeter fridge? Normal. Bakery trip every day? Normal. Wine at lunch and dinner? Normal. Coke with no ice is normal. Donning a skirt and pointy boots to go to the store is normal. Waiting in line at the post office is normal. Oh, wait, we do that in America too.

Small cars are normal. We're already discussing what vehicle we'll buy when we return to the US. I want a little car except I fear getting squashed like a bug by all the SUV's and pickups. I've seen a total of three pickup trucks here. Teenagers in France drive fast with their music thumping loud just like teenagers in the states. Boys check out the girls and the girls like being checked out. Even old girls like me.

Babies cry and kids laugh. Whining sounds like whining whether in French or English. Toddlers climb out of grocery carts and parents swat diapered bottoms. Cell phones are everywhere and although against the law to talk and drive, I see it all the time. I did see something today that was a first. Two worker guys in a white van (all worker guys have white vans) were eating sandwiches while driving.

That may not be against the law, but it smacks French tradition with a crusty baguette.

I haven't started smoking, but second hand smoke is second nature. Fumeur or non-fumeur section doesn't matter. Smoke doesn't stay in its assigned seat. I didn't think it possible, but I've gotten used to it. I barely recall an entire restaurant being no smoking. It'll be interesting to see if that ever happens in France. I've learned never say never, but France will be the last bastion of smokers on earth.

We have witnessed some radical change in our short time here. One of the local grocery stores extended its hours to 9 a.m. to 8 p.m. sans interruption. No midday closing and open past six. Wow. The other store in town followed suit a couple months later. Oh la la. What will happen next? Stores open on Sunday? Open 24 hours? I can't predict, but I like getting groceries over the lunch hour. I'm the only one in the store.

Change is inevitable, even in France. I've learned I must always keep learning and be open to new possibilities. No matter what country I live in.

Grandma O

(May, 2006)

જ∼જી

Old age ain't for sissies the saying goes, but
Grandma O was one tough cookie. Strong and sweet.
Sweet was the word used over and over to describe her.
The good, genuine kind of sweet, not the fake, make your
skin crawl kind.

Even in her last months when she was unable to talk,
the nurses still called Grandma O sweet. Her body was
confined to a hospital bed and hooked up to a myriad of
tubes and machines, but her personality still got through.

Grandma O had a bit of sass too. She told jokes that
I can't repeat here. She was an upbeat positive person and
not a complainer. Several years ago she was in the hospital
for something I don't remember, but I recall visiting her on
New Year's Day.

Entering her room, I was greeted with her big Green
Bay Packer slippers sticking out under the sheets. She
smiled that the nurses were wonderful and the food wasn't
so bad either. She didn't gripe about a ruined holiday or

starting out the new year in a hospital. Her attitude made a lasting impression on me.

Grandma O's house was food, fun, and games. The only time the table wasn't completely covered in food was when we were playing cards or games like Yahtzee. Our favorite game was Pots, simultaneous solitaire with each player flipping furiously through their deck to play on the aces thrown out in the middle and be the first to get rid of their Pots pile. It's a fast paced game. Grandma O with her crooked fingers rarely won, but she always played. When we beat her to a card, she'd call us names like "worm" and "dirty rotten Rockefeller."

Besides being a Packer fan, she followed baseball too. She watched bowling every week. In the glory days of the Chicago Bulls, Grandma O would be glued to her TV, wearing her Scottie Pippen jersey. A Super Bowl party at Grandma O's was a rowdy affair. I doubt I'll watch sports if I'm widowed, but I hope to foster that same sense of fun.

I picture her old kitchen. The gold wallpaper, the copper tile backsplash, the macramé plant hanger, the plaque that says, "There's no place like home, except Grandma's." For holiday meals, she put up a table in the corner to hold overflow food and a card table as the kids' table. Grandma, Mom, and aunts would cram around the table and the men would eat on TV trays in the living room. It was a welcome rite of passage to join the ladies at the real table.

Christmas Eve was my favorite night. I see the eats, drinks, and the big old punch bowl. I see the plastic mistletoe hanging between the kitchen and living room. I see the Christmas cards taped to the back of her front door. I see the red ball ornaments hanging from the light over the kitchen table. I see the tree with the chocolates she tied on for us to eat. I see Rudolph's red nose blinking way far off in the clear cold sky as I stand on her front porch as a little girl.

When my cousin Amy was young, she declared when she grew up and had a baby girl, she would name her Grandma O. That didn't happen of course. None of us named a baby Grandma O or Florence. Her full name was Florence Lorraine Olmstead; her initials and license plate read FLO.

Grandma O died April 23. We'll miss her dearly, but her essence lives on. Her sense of humor and love of life are her enduring legacy. Thanks Grandma O for making each of us feel loved and special. With you, it was true: There's no place like home, except Grandma's.

I Want To Remember Every Little Thing

(June, 2006)

❧

"We may never pass this way again...." I hear Seals and Crofts singing in my head as our days in France wind down. I want to soak it all up, every little thing. My photos will preserve memories of trips, places, and people. I want to capture the unseen feelings, put them in a French apothecary bottle, and crack it open whenever I need a mood boost.

This year was my unpaid sabbatical from minivan mom existence, and I'm richer for the experience. I've researched, studied and traveled. I've made new friends and kept the old. The internet has become my cherished pal, keeping me in touch.

With my trusty laptop and email address book, I'd love to bounce around Europe, living in different places. Germany, Austria, Spain, England, Netherlands, Belgium. All on company expense, of course. Such an opportunity doesn't exist and The Man of the Place has decided he's not an International Man of Mystery. He wants to go home.

I'll savor the days and store the details so I can travel back in my mind. As I walk into town to do errands, I notice hanging wisteria, roses bursting through gates and over walls, and roundabouts teeming with dozens of flower varieties. Flowers are everywhere, and although it can't be true, the colors seem more vibrant. Fresh flowers will be a French habit I'm taking home. Buy a cheap bouquet for your table. Bet you a baguette, it'll make you smile.

Walking to La Poste is one hour round trip. In Illinois, I lived one minute from the grocery store and I drove. People here walk even in the rain. The French use a marvelous invention called an umbrella. I don't hoof it in inclement weather, but usually the sun is shining, sky is blue, and birds are singing, loudly, I might add, so walking is enjoyable. Pedestrians have the right of way and cars stop. And here, a whistle, a honk, or a look of approval from a man is not disrespectful, it's a show of appreciation and a welcome compliment.

My attitude has vacillated from being the queen tourist always carrying my camera to wanting to acclimate and live like a local. I should have stuck with the tourist approach. One day outside the market stood an organ grinder in a straw hat. He didn't have a monkey, but I was wishing I had my camera. Four crinkled old ladies sitting on a bench looked stereotypical French and if I'd had my Kodak, I would've snapped them for posterity. Old men, wearing black berets in the summer, play *boules* in the park. That's a quintessential image I need to keep. I've gone back to toting my camera.

My journal writing has been lax so I fear I'll forget these unexpected delights. As I go about my haus frau duties, I love the surprises that remind me I'm a stranger in a strange land. I'll remember the big events and embarrassing moments, but I also want the nuances to stay with me.

I want to remember the sense of accomplishment I felt when I could understand the question the cashier asked me. I want to remember the calm I felt as I gazed at the orange twilight sky as the cool breeze blew through the house after a hot day. I want to remember the elation I felt strutting the streets of Toulouse after my first creative writing group.

I want to ensnare these emotions and tap into them when I need a fix of "natural high." Perhaps I've found what the French call la joie de vie, the joy of life. Joy doesn't exist only in France. It's also made in the USA. Sometimes it takes a little effort to slow down and let it seize me. I realize that I may never pass this way again. I want to soak it all up, every little thing.

A Man, His Wife, and Modern Technology

(August, 2006)

છ્જ

Another woman has come between me and The Man of the Place. She's sleek, petite and curvy. I understand the attraction. However, I don't appreciate his infatuation or his need to bring her along everywhere.

"She" is not really a woman, but has a female voice. "She" is my husband's GPS. GPS stands for Global Positioning System or Satellite or Something Like That. I gave her a real name. Greta was the first "G" name that came to mind. Greta Please Shut up is her full name.

Greta chatters nonstop. "In 400 feet, enter roundabout. Take third exit." As we approach, she repeats. "In 200 hundred feet, enter roundabout. Take third exit." In case we weren't listening, she tells us again. "Take third exit." If we don't go her way, she says, "Off route; recalculating." Once I think I heard her say, "It's my way or the highway."

The Man of the Place loves her. She fits in the palm of his hand and he finds her totally sexy. I find her annoying. After our first trip with Greta, I was ready to hurl her out the window. I wanted to chuck the Man of the Place, but Greta's an easier toss. The route we needed to take was obvious. I had a map. There was a road sign. I knew where to go. Greta was telling us to take a little dirt road into oblivion. The Man of the Place wanted to give Greta the benefit of the doubt. I wanted to give them both the heave-ho.

Determining the best route from Point A to Point B is not hard with common sense, maps, and road signs. A man does not need GPS and my hubby does not need Greta. Greta would have met an early demise, but one rainy midnight we drove around and around trying to find the Hotel Amadeus in Haarlem, Holland. My directions only said "on the market square." Greta suddenly came in handy and guided us to the hotel.

I agreed to give Greta a break. Our travels established a pattern. Greta would stay on silent mode until we got to our destination town. Then we'd turn up her volume and she'd direct us down roads and up alleys no wider than our van (with the mirrors tucked in). Occasionally we would turn prematurely and have to loop around one ways and squeeze through narrow streets. Greta's patient monotone "In 200 feet turn right" would keep us from wandering into the next country and eventually we'd locate our hotel.

I allowed Greta to stay in our lives and the Man of the Place now realizes she has her flaws. Without maps programmed into her, she's useless. "Drive 100 miles and arrive at destination." Gee, thanks for the help. She loses satellite reception quite often, but she still doesn't shut up. "Lost satellite reception." She's supposed to stick to the windshield, but she falls down a lot. And she doesn't even drink wine.

Gadgets can be fun, but a living, breathing female human with a map on her lap and the ability to read road signs is just as accurate. A female driving partner can carry on a conversation. A three by six inch rectangle cannot. Think about it. Who will be going into the hotel with the man? If he ignores my advice and listens to Greta, he does so at his own risk. The GPS has a mute button. Women do not.

The End Of The Road

(August 2006)

I suffer from post-party depression. My motto: may the fun never end. We're back in Illinois after a year in France. Everyone asks, "Are you glad to be back?" The Man of the Place and my boys answer an unequivocal "Yes." I hesitate. It's rude to respond to a hearty "Welcome back" with "Gee, I wish I wasn't here." That's not exactly true. I don't expect sympathy or understanding. My mixed emotions are something I need to sort out for myself.

I miss the overall thrill of being in Europe and the travel opportunities. I miss little things like wonderful, inexpensive wine and the best bread in the world. I miss the old juxtaposed with the new. I miss folks who became valued friends.

My kids tease me as I order a "Coca" here and the waitress looks at me funny. I want to "bonjour" and "merci" everyone. I want to kiss kiss both cheeks when I greet people. I want to retain what little French I acquired, and keep our Britishspeak. We say some things in jest, but Brit phrases just pop out. We miss those British boys.

I want to talk about France, but some people just aren't interested. If I mention being in Germany or Italy, I don't want to come off as bragging. Or perhaps maybe I am a snob and I need to deal with that. Being abroad for a year has opened my mind. Coming back has opened my eyes too.

Culture shock happens even when one returns to their home country. My sons and I went to the grocery store. We felt empty-handed not bringing bags or taking a cart into the store with us. The choices of candy, cereal and chips were overwhelming and seemed unnecessary. The ketchup bottles were gargantuan. Not having to weigh my own produce and having someone bag our items for us seemed odd.

The French have big grocery stores as well, but have a worshipful reverence for food. They do not snack between meals. They drink red wine. They walk and cycle. They smoke. Whatever the cause, the men look good in their Speedos. I went to the water park here the other day. Not one Speedo in sight, thank goodness. Makes you shudder just thinking about big bellied Americans in tiny little spandex, doesn't it?

One afternoon at the mall here revealed more fat, sloppy women than I'd seen in a year. The newspapers are right. America is an obese nation. French women don't get fat and French women dress more feminine. A gal at the hotel here had on an extremely short skirt and high platform shoes that she could barely walk in. Her tacky outfit and mismatched jewelry looked cheap, not attractive. Showing skin can be done tastefully. And if you can't walk in the heels, leave them at home.

Driving here is boring. It took a week for me to not reach for the clutch when starting my car. My Chevy Impala seemed huge and parking spaces are like landing pads for the space shuttle. You don't have to pay attention to drive. Straight roads. Traffic lights. Scenery is fast food places and big box stores. My thoughts wandered to how I missed the tight, curvy roads, the roundabouts, and fields of sunflowers. I almost hit a car.

That brought me back to reality. I'll adjust to life here again. I'll miss certain aspects of European culture and I'll always be grateful for the experience. It's best to leave the party while still having fun. If it results in a post-party low, that's okay. The highs were worth it.

When Life Stinks, It's Time To Wash The Gym Clothes

(November, 2006)

৵৽৹

I've tried to be patient and nurturing, but once again, the Mother of the Year award has slipped from my grasp. What is my offense? I call my children names. Well, I couch it so it seems like I'm not actually labeling them, but you decide.

"Get off your butts right now and turn off the TV! I will not raise lazy slobs!" What do you think? Did I just call my boys lazy slobs?

They rotate from TV to computer to X-Box and back again, passing by trails of dirty socks and stepping over book bags, but they don't pick anything up. When I asked them to tidy up the drinks and wrappers strewn about the family room, I got blank stares and a reply of "Pick up what stuff?"

Their laundry piles rival the height of the Leaning Tower of Pisa. We visited Italy and discovered that as famous landmarks go, the crumbling Pisa bell tower is not that tall, but if we're talking mounds of dirty clothes, then it's up there. If the heap is higher than a standard refrigerator and ready to topple, it's a Pisa and I don't want it in my home.

My older son has laundry hamper phobia. He leaves all his clothes on the bathroom floor. In a moment of patient nurturing (it washes over me occasionally), I moved his hamper to the bathroom so he would not have to walk the five steps to his bedroom to deposit his dirty dirties. His clothes still lay on the bathroom floor, physically touching the hamper, but not in it.

I've told him repeatedly that clothes not in the hamper will not get washed. Yes, I realize that I can pick his clothes up off the floor just as easily as if they were in the white plastic basket, but it's the principle of the thing. Boys need to learn "mother" is not synonymous for "maid."

Elder son will now sometimes run out of clean necessary items. I smile sweetly and say, "Everything in the laundry basket gets washed." He smiles sweetly and raids his dad's or brother's drawers for clean socks and t-shirts.

Now that basketball season has started, both boys come home and dump their school clothes and smelly practice gear on the family room floor. Some stinky stuff makes its way to the kitchen, some on the stairs to the basement, some on the stairs going up to the bedrooms. Clothes are strewn everywhere. My sons however just sit and stare at the TV, oblivious to it all. When did my babies become men?

It was my plan that once my boys were in high school, they would have to do their own laundry. I may start early. If a kid is taller than his mom and wears more clothes in any given day than a New York runway model, then it may be time for him to learn the finer points of a Maytag.

High school may be a year away, but Laundry 101 starts today. A child who can download Comedy Central shows onto his I-pod can certainly learn how to run a washing machine. Sorting whites, darks, and everything in between may prove a challenge, but I tell my guys that life is hard. Life is not always fair. And when life stinks, it's time to wash your gym clothes.

My guys are growing up and I have much to teach them still. One lesson to learn is the old adage: Nothing is certain in life, but death, taxes and laundry.

Kelly Meredith Epperson

After the events of September 11, 2001, I wrote thank-you notes to various people for various reasons. Among those who wrote back was Dave Barry. His handwritten postcard simply stated: "Thanks, and good luck with your column. Your fellow humorist, Dave Barry." The card still has a place of honor on my bulletin board, next to my Live Aid ticket stub, and a cartoon dog that says, "I'm so happy I could pee."

I've learned that we cannot predict life, and I've learned that I'm still so happy I could pee. My days consist of writing and speaking gigs. I get to dress up in cute skirts (occasionally a boa and tiara too) and make people laugh. I'm grateful.

I'm a member of AHA (American Happiness Association), AATH (Association for Applied and Therapeutic Humor) and NSNC (National Society of Newspaper Columnists. I was a panel judge for the 2010 Erma Bombeck National Essay Contest; I've started the Happiness Club of Loves Park, IL; my boys are now teenagers, and I still like dancing alone in my kitchen.

Staying in touch with readers brings me joy. Sign up for a free weekly happy email at www.kellyepperson.com. My life continues to evolve and I've learned it really is about JOY - the Journey of You. Learn with me at www.journeyofyou.com.

Kelly Epperson
PO Box 2324
Loves Park IL 61131
kel_epperson@yahoo.com
815-871-7864

D0001540

These columns have previously appeared in various newspapers owned by Rock Valley Publishing and Eagle Publications.

Cover design by Susan Daffron, Logical Expressions, Inc.
Cover Photo by Kelly Epperson
I'll gladly go back to the hilltop village of Cordes sur Ciel to ask photo use permission of the unidentified French man hanging out laundry. I was the only person in France who used a clothes dryer. My thousands of photos from our year abroad include one of my French washer and dryer, but it's not as charming as this photo. Merci beaucoup, monsieur.

ISBN: 978-0-9827667-1-2

Library of Congress Control Number: 2008926418

Kelly began writing her column in May 2001, and has gathered a large and loyal readership.
Here's a sample from her mailbag:

"When the paper comes, I go directly to your column. You're a hoot."
  ~Debbie Westervelt

"You are amazing. I love reading everything you write. Words can't describe how great your writing makes others feel."
  ~Tanya Edmundson

"I enjoyed reading about your adventures in France. My family moved to Sweden for a year, and I now feel as if I belong in two worlds. I get that same feeling from your writings and I am glad to know these feelings are shared. I look forward to reading your columns, and lycker till (good luck) in your writing career."
  ~ Barry Smith

"Thanks for writing such enthusiastic columns. You write best when it comes from the heart."
  ~ Alan Stolldorf

"I began reading way before you ever headed off to Europe and became a fan right from the start. Your wit is charming and delightful to read."
  ~Sharon Shirk

"Thanks so much for sharing. Keep on writing; your articles are truly the best part of the paper!"
  ~ Christine Holmes

"Your columns are beautiful and inspirational. I cut them out to keep."
  ~ Bonnie Staas

"Is it weird to say I love you? You make me smile. Clever, silly, insightful, dedicated. You make EVERYone happy when you are happy!
  ~Mary Lamphere